Stunting

A CHEER-TECHnique Book

Glenn Kingsbury

authorHOUSE®

AuthorHouse™
1663 Liberty Drive
Bloomington, IN 47403
www.authorhouse.com
Phone: 1-800-839-8640

Kingsbury, Glenn
Drew, Karen

Published by AuthorHouse   09/19/2012

ISBN: 978-1-4490-4832-7 (sc)
ISBN: 978-1-4490-4834-1 (e)

Library of Congress Control Number: 2012905703

Cover and design by Ken Drew, ikendrew design
Layout by Karen Drew
Edited by Karen Drew and Shana Hart
Photography by Karen Drew and Angel Ryker

This book is dedicated to my mom, Elaine Ann Kingsbury. If it wasn't for her encouraging me to follow my dreams I would never have become the person I am today. Her love and devotion drove me to the path that I chose and I owe my success to her and my Father, John Franklin Kingsbury. They both taught me that hard work and dedication will help you get through anything.

Special thanks to Joel Baba's Gymnastics School for allowing us to use their school and athletes to put this book together and Ed Gardner for getting the athletes together. I would like to thank Shana Hart for her help editing and critiquing this book. Plus I would like to thank Karen Drew for her help with finishing touches on this book. And lastly I need to thank Ken Drew for the cover design, artwork throughout the book, and layout design and to Angel Ryker and Karen Drew for taking the pictures necessary to fill the pages of the book.

Foreward

My name is Glenn Kingsbury and I am the owner and CEO of Cheer Tech. I have been in the cheerleading industry as for more than 20 years now. I have been a cheerleader, a coach of several college teams, as well as owning an all star program and gym. I have taught cheer camps and clinics for 20 years as well. The purpose behind writing this book was to help educate the cheerleaders and their coaches with the same knowledge that I use when teaching camps and clinics.

Table of Contents:

INTRODUCTION

STUNTING

Introduction

Fundamentals

When learning how to perform cheerleading stunts, here are some basic concepts that will help you use this book and stunt effectively and safely. A stunt group is usually composed of either 3,4, or 5 people. Each person should be selected for their position based on height, weight, flexibility, and strength.

The first position is the Back Spot, this person stands at the back of MOST stunts. The Back Spot is typically the tallest member of the group.

The second position would be the Base Position; there can be either one or two of them. If the stunt has only one Base, in most cases the Base stands behind the Flyer and adjacent to the Back Spot. If you are using two, both Bases typically stand face to face with each other, and in front of the Back Spot.

The next position is the Flyer, and the Flyer typically starts with their back to the Back spot, and between the Bases.

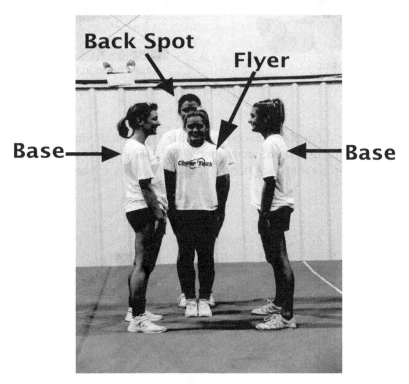

Multiple Base Stunts
Positions - No Front Spot

When the positions are all assembled in their stunt group and ready to build, this is called the Set or Ready Position. When the Flyer begins the stunt and enters into the first position this is called the Load or Mount. When the Flyer executes the stunt, we say that the stunt has Hit. And lastly when the Flyer is coming out of the stunt and it is solid it is called the Dismount.

For every stunt there are corresponding hand positions for the Bases. For most multi-based stunts here is a breakdown of how to hold the Flyer's feet.

*Position 1 the Bases hands are placed under the Flyer's foot, palms up with fingertips pointing forward. With the front hand holding the underside of the Flyer's toe, and the back hand holding the underside of the Flyer's heel.

Position 1

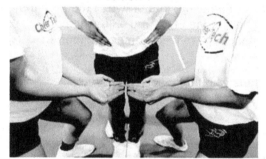

Bases' hand are set for Position 1
Bases' are placed at hip level

Position 1

Base's hand in Position 1. Front hand grabs under Toe, back hand grabs under heel

*Position 2 the Bases' hands are placed under the Flyer's foot, palms up with the heel of the Bases' hands pointing toward each other. The Bases' front hand and fingertips grip the Flyer's toe and the Bases' back hand grips the Flyer's toe heel.

Position 2

Base's hand are in Position 2
Arms are Close to chest and under foot.

The fourth position is the Front Spot, this person is used to help stabilize the stunt, for more power, and safety. They typically stand in the front of the stunt group facing the Flyer.

Multiple Base Stunts
Positions - With Front Spot
Side View

The fifth position is the Pole or Post, this position is like the Front Spot but is used in Single Base stunts to assist the Base with the stunt, and typically stand directly in front of the Base. The Pole can also become the Back Spot for certain stunts.

The last position is the Toe Pitch, this position is used to also assist the Base in Single Base stunts, but stands next to the Base. The Toe Pitch grabs the foot of the Flyer to assist in lifting the Flyer.

Single Base with a Pole

Single Base with a Toe Pitch

Single Base Stunts
Positions

Back Spot

Base

Flyer

In this book we have included many of the possible beginner to elite stunts that are possible to execute. Keep in mind that there are variations that can be executed once the basics are mastered. On that note, we have also included one version of how to build and execute each stunt. The method we chose may not be what you are familiar with so check with your coaches/organization to see if they have a preferred method. It is good to know all methods and tweak them to fit your athletes/program. Most importantly when attempting the skills in this book, please make sure that you perform a proper stretch and execute all skills on a safe surface. DO NOT attempt the harder skills until you have mastered the basics. In addition, always have extra spotters available and ready to step in when you are trying something new. This is not meant as a substitute to having a coach present, but instead a resource to expand your knowledge of how to build and execute different stunts.

On another note in this book we have elected to use "one side" (Left or Right) to execute the skills. It is indicated in the description of the stunt as to which side we are using. It is possible to use the other side just change the side and convert the other steps accordingly. Either way is acceptable and both ways should be practiced to help the Flyer master all skills. In addition we also have used a Front Spot for some stunts. A Front Spot is typically optional for most stunts but if you are a beginner stunter, having a Front Spot increases safety. There are also some instances where a Front Spot is used without a lot of explanation of their role. Typically they will assist the Flyer in building by holding the shin/foot of the Flyer not getting in the way of the Bases. Then during the execution of the stunt they help with the stunt and dismount. For Dismounts the Flyer should be careful to move to the side to avoid getting hit by the feet of the Flyer while assisting in the catch. In some stunt explanations, a Front Spot may not be illustrated but may be used in that stunt.

This book has been written to help educate cheerleaders, coaches, and/or advisors in the proper way to start, build, and complete different stunts. The book begins with thigh stands and goes through 1 and 2 footed stunts, dismounts, and co-ed or partner stunts. When using this book please start in the beginning of a chapter before moving onto harder stunts later on in the chapter. Harder skills rely on some information that is taught in the first few pages and is only breezed through in the harder skills. In addition, we have indicated at the top of each skill a difficulty level; please use this as a guide as you progress with your team/program. Do not try the harder more elite skills until you have mastered the beginner skills, proper technique, safety, and execution of the stunts. On the right hand side of the first page of each stunt there are megaphones indicating the level of difficulty for that particular stunt.

Here is the breakdown of difficulty

 Beginner skill; appropriate for all levels

 Intermediate skill; appropriate for most levels

 Advance skill; appropriate for higher level – requires more body strength and control, additional spotters are highly recommended at this level

 Elite skill; appropriate for advance level only – should only be attempted when other skills have been mastered and using additional spotters is a must at this level when learning.

At the end of the book is a glossary to look up terms as you come across them in the book. Also at the end of the book is an appendix with additional pictures and terms to facilitate learning.

THIGH STANDS

1.

STUNTING

Stunt Explanation

Base

Base sets into a side lunge position (direction optional). When Flyer puts her foot into Base's hip pocket, Base secures foot. Base's outside hand grips over Flyer's foot, fingers under toe, base's inside arm goes around the leg from behind and wraps above the Flyer's knee. The tighter the wrap is, the more stable the stunt will be.

Flyer

Flyer places inside foot into the hip pocket of the Base. Flyer places hands on Base's shoulders. On count, the Flyer will push through her arms (which are pushing on Bases shoulders) to help lock her leg out. This is referred to as **Step, Lock, Tighten (SLT).** Once leg is locked, the Flyer will lift the outside leg up to Liberty position and hit end position with arms, in this case a High V.

Note: Flyer can use 1 or both hands on either of Base's shoulder to push.

Back Spot

Back Spot will hold the Flyer's waist. On count, the Back Spot will assist the Flyer into the stunt and will not let go until Flyer has dismounted safely to performance surface.

Dismount

The Flyer lowers leg and steps off the front of the stunt in a controlled manor. The Base releases Flyer's leg and grabs the Flyer's waist for dismount. The Back Spot remains holding the Flyer's waist and follows Flyer's as Flyer steps off the stunt. Base and Back Spot do not let go until the Flyer is safely on the ground.

Single Based Thigh Stand

Positions

1. Lunge

2. Hip Pocket

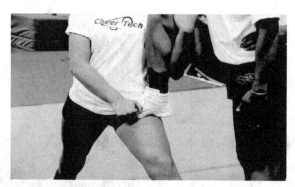

3. Base pulls Flyer's foot in hip pocket

4. Base's Left Hand holds above Knee

5. Base's Right Hand holds Flyers Toe

Single Based Thigh Stand

Technique

1. Set grip - Flyer's hand on Base's shoulder, Base gripping Flyer's foot and knee. Note: 2 hands may be used on Base's shoulder

2. On count, Flyer pushes off Base's shoulder and locks leg out. **Step Lock Tighten**

3. Flyer executes Liberty position by pulling up free leg

4. Dismount - Flyer straightens lifted leg and steps off front

5. Back Spot assists landing

6. Flyer stands in front of Base

Stunt Explanation

Bases

Right Base stands on the Flyer's right side, and Left Base stands on Flyer's left side. The Bases will line their front feet up, one in front of the other in a lunge position with Bases' toes pointed toward each other. Flyer steps into Right Base's Hip Pocket. Right Base's outside or Right hand is placed under the Flyer's toe. Right Base places Base's left arm under Flyer's leg and grabs above the Flyer's right knee for support.

Left Base grabs Flyer's left foot, when Flyer steps into Hip Pocket. Left Base uses left hand to support under Flyer's Left Toe, and Left Base's Right arm under Flyer's leg and grabs above the Flyer's left knee for support.

Flyer

Flyer places both hands on Bases' shoulders. The Flyer will step right foot into Right Base's Hip Pocket and locks foot in. On count, Flyer will **Step, Lock, Tighten (SLT)** and place Left foot into Left Base's Hip Pocket, locking out left leg and standing up straight. Flyer then hits end position such as a High V.

Back Spot

Back Spot grabs the waist of the Flyer and provide support to the Flyer in the stunt. Back Spot will keep hands on the Flyer at all times and is responsible for helping Flyer onto and off of the stunt safely.

Dismount

Both Bases take their outside hand off of the Flyer's Toe and grab the Flyer's hands. On count, Flyer steps off the front of the stunt. Bases take their inside hands and grab Flyer's arms (as close to armpit as possible) with fingers forward to help the Flyer to the ground safely. The Back stays hands-on throughout the entire stunt.

Double Base Thigh Stand

Positions

1. Lunge

2. Hip Pocket

3. Base pulls Flyers foot in hip pocket

4. Base's Left Hand holds above Knee

5. Both Bases holding Flyer

Double Base Thigh Stand
Technique

1. Flyer steps into pocket of Base 1. Flyer's Hands on Both Base's Shoulders

2. On count, Flyer pushes off Base's shoulder and Step, Lock, and Tighten Leg 1

3. Flyer places other leg in other Base's Hip Pocket. Base 2 wraps above knee and supports toe

4. Option - Bases can let go of toe and hit arm position

5. Dismount - Bases' outside arms grab Flyer's hands

6. On count, Bases pop flyer and grab under armpits fingers forward for for extra support and control

7. Bases support in landing

Stunt Explanation

Base

The Base sets into a lunge position (direction optional). As Flyer steps in, the Base pulls the Flyer's left foot into Base's left Hip Pocket. The Base will support the Flyer's toe with Base's outside arm while using inside arm to wrap around back of leg, supporting Flyer's leg above the knee. On count, Flyer will lift the other leg to an L position, behind Base's head. Base will release Flyer's toe and reach for the ankle of the Flyer's other leg (the one behind Base's head) to support Flyer's leg in an "L" position.

Flyer

Flyer places hands on Base's shoulders. Flyer will step into Base's Hip Pocket and **Step, Lock, Tighten (SLT)** with one leg. On count, Flyer pushes through shoulders of Base. On count, Flyer lifts opposite leg into L position behind Base's head. Arm position for the Flyer is an L position in same direction of leg.

Back Spot

The Back Spot is hands-on throughout the entire stunt. Back Spot grabs Flyer's waist. On count, the Back Spot will help lift and balance the Flyer keeping hands on the Flyer's waist.

Dismount

Base moves the Flyer's leg off the front of the stunt to allow the Flyer to step off the front. Back Spot maintains contact with Flyer's waist and assists with the landing. Back Spot does not let the Flyer go until the Flyer is safely on the ground. The Base will also help with the landing.

L Thigh Stand
Positions

1. Lunge

2. Hip Pocket

3. Base pulls Flyer's foot in Hip Pocket

4. Base's Left Hand holds above Flyer's Knee

5. Base's Right Hand holds Flyer's Toe

L Thigh Stand

Technique

1. Set grip - Flyer's hand on Base's shoulder

2. On count, Flyer pushes off Base's shoulder and locks leg out. **Step, Lock, Tighten**

3. Flyer lifts back leg behind Base's head to L position. Base extends same arm as Flyer's Leg and supports L Position

4. Dismount - Base moves Flyer's Leg off front and Flyer steps off front

5. Back Spot assists landing

6. Flyer stands in front of Base

Stunt Explanation

Base

The Base sets into a lunge position (direction optional). As the Flyer steps in, the Base pulls the Flyer's inside foot into Base's Hip Pocket. The Base will support the Flyer's toe with Base's outside arm while using inside arm to wrap around back of leg, supporting the leg above the knee of the Flyer.

Flyer

Flyer places both hands on Base's shoulders. The Flyer will step into the Base's Hip Pocket and **Step, Lock, and Tighten(SLT)** with inside leg. On count, the Flyer will push through the shoulders of the Base and pull up with other leg. On count Flyer will hit Heel Stretch position and with opposite arm hit the

Back Spot

The Back Spot is hands-on throughout the entire stunt. Back Spot starts by grabbing the waist of the Flyer. On count, the Back Spot will help lift and balance the Flyer keeping hands on Flyer's waist.

Dismount

Flyer lowers leg to dead leg position and steps off the front. The Base will help with the landing. Back Spot assists with the landing also, and does not let the Flyer go until the Flyer is safely on the ground.

Heel Stretch Thigh Stand
Positions

1. Lunge

2. Hip Pocket

3. Base pulls Flyer's foot in hip pocket

4. Base's Left Hand holds above Flyer's Knee

5. Base's Right Hand holds Flyer's Toe

Heel Stretch Thigh Stand

Technique

1. Set grip - Flyer's hand on Base's shoulder, Base gripping Flyer's foot and knee

2. On count, Flyer pushes off Base's shoulder and locks leg out. **Step, Lock, Tighten**

3. Flyer executes Heel Stretch by pulling up free leg. Opposite arm extends to end position

4. Dismount - Flyer lowers lifted leg and steps off front

5. Back Spot assists landing

6. Flyer stands in front of Base

Stunt Explanation

Base

The Base sets into a lunge position (direction optional). As Flyer steps in, the Base pulls the Flyer's outside foot into the Base's Hip Pocket. The Base will support the Flyer's toe with Base's outside arm while using inside arm to wrap around back of leg, supporting Flyer's leg above the knee. On count, Flyer will lift the opposite leg over the Base's shoulder. Base stands up and wraps hands above the Flyer's knees for support.

Note: Right Lunge is to Flyer's Right Foot; Left Lunge is to Flyer's Left Foot.

Flyer

Flyer places hands on Base's shoulders. The Flyer will step into Base's Hip Pocket. On count, Flyer will push through shoulders of Base and **Step, Lock, Tighten(SLT)** with one leg. Flyer will then lift opposite leg over the Base's shoulder and sit on Base's shoulders. For best support, the Flyer squeezes her legs and top of shoelaces into Base's kidneys.

Back Spot

Back Spot grabs Flyer's waist. The Back Spot remains hands-on throughout the entire stunt. On count, the Back Spot will support the Flyer until the Flyer is stable in the shoulder sit, keeping hands on Flyer's waist.

Dismount

See Next 2 pages for Dismount Techniques.

Shoulder Sit

Positions

1. Lunge

2. Hip Pocket

3. Base pulls Flyer's foot in Hip Pocket

4. Base's Left Hand holds above Flyer's Knee

5. Flyer locks legs around behind Base and squeezes top of shoelaces into Base's Back

Shoulder Sit

Technique

1. Set grip - Flyer's hand on Base's shoulders

2. On count, Flyer pushes off Base's shoulder and Flyer locks leg out.
Step, Lock, Tighten

3. Once Flyer's leg is locked out Flyer lifts opposite leg over Base's shoulder

4. Base grabs Flyer's legs above the knees. Back Spot holds Flyer's waist

Stunt Explanation

Intermediate/Advanced
Dismount
Dismount Off Front

Flyer straightens one leg and grabs the Base's hand on the outside of Flyer's Leg. When secure, repeat on opposite side. On count, the Base dips and drives through her legs with arms upward and drives Flyer above Base's head to free Flyer from sit position. The Flyer's arms remain locked and pressed down through Bases' arms. Flyer floats off the front with feet together. Back Spot remains hands on as much as possible, and follows around the front of the stunt to assist with the landing.

Beginner/Intermediate
Dismount
Dismount Off Back

Flyer straightens one leg and grabs the Base's hand between Flyer's legs. When secure, repeat for opposite side. On count, the Base dips and shrugs Flyer off the back. Flyer performs a reverse toe touch off Base and holds Base's hands the entire time.
Back Spot grabs waist and helps lower Flyer to landing as Base maintains hand grip with Flyer and dips down so Base is not pulled down.

Shoulder Sit
Technique
Dismount Off Front

1. Flyer grabs one hand of Base on outside of Flyer's leg

2. Flyer grabs other hand of Base on outside of Flyer's leg

3. Base squats, Back Spot moves to side of Base and supports Flyer's Back

4. Base extends arms and thrusts head through legs to free Flyer from sit position

5. Flyer presses through hands and dismounts feet first to floor

6. Back Spot assists Flyer with landing

Shoulder Sit

1. Flyer straightens Right Leg and Base grabs Flyer's Right hand between Flyer's legs

2. Flyer straightens Left Leg and Base grabs Flyer's Left hand between Flyer's legs

3. **Side View** Flyer straightens Left Leg and Base grabs Flyer's Left hand between Flyer's legs

4. Base squats

5. On count, Base squats and shrugs Flyer off Back

6. Flyer straddles off back of Base and brings feet together for landing. Base holds Flyer's hands the entire time

7. Base squats on landing with Flyer so Base is not yanked backwards

Stunt Explanation

Base

The Base lunges into either a double lunge or a side lunge (both are acceptable). The Base will reach backward with her arms, elbows near her ears and grab the Flyer's hands. The Flyer steps into Base's Hip Pocket as Base locks arms above Base's head. Flyer Steps, Locks, and Tightens leg and raises opposite Foot to the Base's shoulder (on the same side as the foot- left to left, etc). The Base stands and the Flyer places the other foot (the one on the Base's thigh) on the opposite shoulder. The Base lets right hand go and grabs Flyer's calf (high) and pulls downward, repeat with other side. The Base needs to keep head up for support and locks with Flyer's legs.

Flyer

The Flyer grabs the Base's hands. On count, Flyer places foot into Hip Pocket, pushes off shoulders and Step, Lock, Tighten and places other foot on Base's shoulder. The Flyer then places the other foot on Base's opposite shoulder and locks legs outright (foot to right shoulder and left foot to left shoulder). To tighten the position, the Flyer should lock heels together behind Base's head. Flyer will then stand straight after releasing hands with Base and hitting end position such as High V.

Back Spot

The Back Spot helps to power and balance the stunt with hands-on technique. Back Spot starts with hands on waist. As Flyer places foot on Base's shoulder, Back Spot grabs Flyer's upper thigh or ankle, maintaining contact with the Flyer for the entire stunt.

Dismount

Flyer reaches for Base's Right hand and then Left hand. Flyer is then popped off the front of the stunt while Base provides tension to lower Flyer to ground. The Back Spot also moves to the side and grabs Flyer's waist assisting in landing.

Shoulder Stand

1. Flyer sets hand grip by shaking hands with Base. Flyer places foot into Base's hip pocket

2. Flyer pushes down on Base's hip pocket

6. Dismount - Base grabs right hand

7. Base then grabs left hand

Shoulder Stand

3. Flyer will Step, Lock, and Tighten on Base's Thigh. Flyer brings opposite foot to Base's Shoulder and Base locks arms above head

4. Flyer places other foot on Base's shoulder

5. Base grips Flyer's upper calves and pulls down. Flyer releases hands when solid

8. Flyer pops off the front. Base slows Flyer's descent with tension in arms

9. Back Spot slides to side and helps assist landing

10. Back Spot lowers Flyer to floor and finishes on side of Flyer

Stunt Explanation

Bases

Base stands behind Flyer, squatting down and grabbing Flyer's ankles. On count, Flyer dips and jumps and Base drives Flyer's legs up, picking them up above shoulders and placing Flyer's feet on Base's own shoulders. Once on shoulders, Base slides hands to top of calf and pulls down securely.

Flyer

Flyer stands in front of Base and behind Front Spot or "Pole". Flyer grabs Pole's hands in front of Flyer. Flyer's feet are together, and on count, Flyer dips and jumps and locks arms pushing against Pole. Flyer pulls body up through hips and feet land on Base's shoulders. To tighten the position, the Flyer should lock heels together behind Base's head.

Pole

Pole stands in front of Flyer with back facing Flyer. Pole grabs Flyers hands by reaching behind with elbows in. On count, when Flyer jumps, Pole locks arms out keeping biceps near her ears.

Dismount

On count, Base pops Flyer off front of shoulder stand, and regrabs Flyer's waist as Flyer lands. At same time, Pole does half twist to face Flyer to help control landing.

Table Top

1. Set Grip - Base grabs Flyer's ankles

4. Place Feet on Base's shoulders

5. Base locks in Flyer's calves

8. Base follows Flyer down, grabbing waist of Flyer

Table Top

2. Flyer and Base squats

3. Base drives from ankles

6. Base squats and slides
   hands down legs

7. Base pops Flyer off front,
   Pole turns 180 degrees into stunt

9. Landing- Base and Flyer Squat,
   Pole keeps holding Flyer's hands

Stunt Explanation

Bases

Base stands behind Flyer squatting down and grabbing Flyer's ankles. On count Flyer jumps and Base drives Flyer's legs up, picking them up above shoulders and placing Flyer's feet on Bases own shoulders. Once on shoulders Base slides hands to top of calf and pulls down aggressively.

Flyer

Flyer stands in front of Base and behind Front Spot or "Pole". Flyer grabs Pole's hands in front of Flyer. Flyer's feet are together, and on count Flyer jumps and locks arms pushing against Pole. Flyer pulls body up through hips and feet land on Base's shoulders. To tighten the position, the Flyer should lock heels together behind Bases head. Flyer will release hands with Pole and stand up straight.

Pole

Pole stands in front of Flyer with back facing Flyer. Pole grabs Flyers hands by reaching behind with elbows in. On count when Flyer jumps Pole locks arms out keeping biceps near her ears. When Flyer is in control, Pole will release hands, one at a time, and turn clockwise and move to the back right corner of Base keeping, visual contact with stunt, for safety.

1. Set Grip - Base grabs Flyers ankles

4. Place Feet on Base's shoulders

5. Base locks in Flyer's calves

Table Top to Shoulder Stand

2. Flyer and Base squats

3. Base drives from ankles

6. Flyer releases hands with Pole.
   Pole moves to back right corner

7. Flyer hits stunt

Stunt Explanation

Bases

The Base lunges into a front lunge. The Base will reach backward with her arms, hands near her ears and grabs the Flyer's hands. The Flyer places foot onto the top of Base's calf. On count, Base squats, pops calf, straightens and locks her arms above head. As Flyer is elevated, Flyer first places one foot, then the other, onto Base's Shoulders (on the same side as the foot-left to left, etc). The Base stands as Flyer places the second foot. The Base lets right hand go and grabs Flyer's calf (high) and pulls downward, repeat with other side. The Base needs to keep head up for support.

Flyer

The Flyer places toe first into the top of the Base's calf. On count, the Base pops calf and Flyer's leg locks-out, while locking arms and driving against the Base to get height. Flyer then places one foot on Base's shoulder. The Flyer then places other foot on opposite shoulder and locks legs out. To tighten the position, the Flyer should lock heels together behind Base's head. Flyer releases hands with Base and straightens to hit end position.

Back Spot

The Back Spot helps to power and balance the stunt with hands-on technique. Back Spot starts with hands on waist and as Flyer places foot on shoulder, grabs Flyer's upper thigh or ankle, maintaining contact with the Flyer for the entire stunt.

Calf Pop

1. Flyer sets grip and foot

2. Flyer and Base squat

3. Base snaps leg. Flyer shoots off leg and pressing off arms

4. Flyer lifts hips and sets right foot on Base's shoulder

5. Flyer hits stunt

43

Stunt Explanation

Bases

Base stands behind Flyer. Base grabs Flyers hands in position 1. On count, Flyer and Base squat, Base and Flyer then flip handgrip to position 2, as Base lifts Flyer upward. Base continues to drive through Base's legs and arms, driving Flyer upward, above Base's head, until Flyer's feet are comfortably on Base's shoulders. Base releases right hand, grabs upper calf, and pulls down. Repeat same for left hand and calf. The Base needs to keep head up for support.

Flyer

Flyer stands with feet together, arms at side with hands behind and palms up, fingers back. Base grabs and connects with Flyer's hand grip. On count, Flyer squats and jumps up flipping handgrip to position 2, flipping the wrists so that Flyer can now push against the Base's hands. If the wrists don't flip, the Flyer will not be able to support her own weight. As Flyer drives through the arms, the Flyer should keep elbows locked, and pull hips up. Flyer keeps weight on arms as much as possible, until feet are able to be placed in the correct position on Base's shoulders. Flyer releases right hand and then left as Base secures legs. To tighten the position, the Flyer should lock heels together behind Base's head, hitting end position.

Back Spot

Back Spot spots back right corner of Base. Back Spot is there to aid and assist if any problems occur.

Purdue Up

Positions

1. Set Grip

2. Hand Position 1

3. Hand Position 2 - Base gets under Flyer

Purdue Up

1. Base and Flyer squat

2. Flyer keeps arms and feet together during drive upward

3. Flyer pulls hips up

4. Flyer settles into Shoulder Stand, placing feet on Base's shoulders

5. Flyer hits end position

Stunt Explanation

Bases

Base will grab Flyer by waist. On count, Base and Flyer will squat. Base throws Flyer upward, driving through legs and extending arms directly above head, snapping at top. After Base snaps, his head should be looking straight forward. Base helps guide Flyer up. Flyer should ride up and land on shoulders where Base will grab tops of calves and pull down.

NOTE - The Difference between this and all other "Throw Tricks" is that Base does not want to look up at Flyer in this trick   Looking up will cause the shoulders to not be in the correct spot for landing and therefore, making the stunt harder as well as dangerous. Make sure to avoid this by looking straight forward.

Flyer

Flyer stands in front of Base, with feet together and grabbing wrists of Base. On count, Flyer will squat leaning on Base ever so lightly. Flyer will jump straight up keeping weight in wrists of Base. After Base releases, Flyer will continue to ride to top and open legs 6-8 inches apart. Flyer will stay tight and settle in, locking feet when feet land on shoulders, Hitting end position–High V.

Back Spot

Back Spot stands at back right corner of Base and is there to assist if any problems occur. Back Spot can also help Flyer by placing one hand on Flyer's Back and the other on Flyer's waist as Flyer jumps.

Throw Shoulder Stand

1. Set grip

2. Flyer and Base squat

3. Base throws Flyer through to top. Base keeps head forward, and hands close to Flyer's legs

4. Base catches and locks calves in by pulling down

5. Flyer hits stunt

Stunt Explanation

Bases
Base and Flyer connect hand positions; right hand to right hand, left hand to left hand. Flyer's right hand shakes Base's right hand, Flyer's left hand grabs Base's left hand with palms in and thumbs down. Flyer places Right foot onto forearm of Base's Right arm. On count, Base will squat and pop forearm. Base will drive Flyer upward, locking arms and above head until Flyer lands with feet on shoulders. During this process, Base keeps arms as close to ears as possible after pop. Base releases right hand, grabs upper calf, and pulls down. Repeat same for left hand and calf. The Base needs to keep his head up for support.

Flyer
Base and Flyer connect hand positions; right hand to right hand, left hand to left hand. Flyer places right foot into forearm of Bases right arm. On count Base squats and drives Flyer up. Flyer will snap off right leg and drive upward twisting hips into same direction as Base, locking and pushing through arms to hips up position, keeping as much weight on Base's arms as possible. Flyer releases right hand and then left as Base secures legs. To tighten the position, the Flyer should lock heels together behind Bases head. Flyer hits end position.

Back Spot
Back Spot will hold Flyer by waist, if needed, to help begin process of snap and to get height and leverage. More advanced stunters may not need this option. Back Spot will then go to back right corner of Base to help with support and safety if needed.

Forearm Pop

1. Set grip

2. Flyer steps onto Base's forearm close to elbow and squats

3. Flyer jumps, Base pulls with left arm and pushes with right arm

4. Base drives through arm, and puts Flyer above Base's head

5. Flyer puts feet on Base's shoulders

6. Flyer hits shoulder stand

2 FOOT STUNTS

STUNTING

Purpose of this stunt is to teach Flyer to hold her own weight during load-ins. This drill should be performed and mastered before moving on. By being able to hold her own body weight, the stunt group will have an easier time learning more difficult

Bases stand facing each other, with the Flyer's hands on the Bases' shoulders, holding the weight of the Flyer.

Flyer places a hand on each Bases' shoulder, elbows up. Elbows up will allow Flyer to get a good push off of the Bases. On count, the Flyer jumps and locks her arms, holding her own weight – hovering in a tuck position. Correct body position is having chest, knees, and toes even, looking forward. After holding for several counts, Flyer returns her feet to the ground.

Back Spot places her hands on the Flyer's waist, assists in the jump and steadies Flyer during Hover. Back Spot then helps Flyer back to the ground safely.

1. Set Position

2. Flyer squats

3. Flyer jumps up and pushes down on Bases' shoulders

4. Flyer pulls knees up and locks arms

5. View from back - Flyer's hips should be held by base and behind Flyer's shoulders

Stunt Explanation

Purpose

Purpose of this drill is to help with timing and precision, for the Bases, Flyer, and Back Spot.

Bases

Bases start facing each other, with legs shoulder width apart, and knees bent. Hands are together, palm up and pinky fingers connected. The Flyer jumps up and pulls legs into a tuck position with all the Flyer's weight in her arms. On count, the Flyer's feet land on the Base's hands. The Bases bounce by squatting and thrusting Flyer out of their hands to return to ground.

Flyer

Flyer places a hand on each Bases' shoulder, elbows up. Elbows up will allow Flyer to get a good push off of the Bases. On count, the Flyer jumps and locks her arms, holding her own weight – hovering in a tuck position. Flyer places a foot into each of the Bases' hands. As Bases squat, Flyer shrugs shoulders and bounces off the back landing on the performing surface.

Back Spot

Back Spot places her hands on the Flyer's waist, assists in the jump, and steadies Flyer during Hover and bounce. Back Spot then helps Flyer back to the ground safely.

Bounce Drill

1. Set Position. Flyer's hands are on Bases' shoulders

2. Flyer and Back Spot squat

6. Bases squat

7. Bases drive up, maintaining an "L" position with their arms. Flyer grabs Back Spot's wrists

3. As Flyer jumps, Flyer supports her own weight on Bases' shoulders

4. Bases catch Flyer's feet

5. Base's catch Flyer's feet (Rear View)

8. Back Spot controls Flyer's descent (Rear View)

9. Back Spot controls Flyer's descent. Bases keep hands at side

10. Back Spot assists in Flyer's landing. Both Flyer and Back Spot bend knees for landing

Stunt Explanation

Bases

Bases start facing each other, with legs shoulder width apart and knees bent. Hands are together, palms up, elbows in by ribcage, (fingertips touching other fingertips). Flyer will put one foot in one Base's hands. On count, Bases squat as the Flyer's other foot goes into other Bases' hands and both Bases drive up to shoulder level. While the Bases are bringing the feet up to shoulder level, they stand up and also switch their grip on the feet. The new grip will be heel & toe known as Position 2– front foot on Flyer's toe and Back hand on Flyer's heel. Bases should get as much of their hands under the Flyers feet as possible. Only the fingertips will wrap the heel and toe. Bases will also keep arms close to their own chests for more support.

Flyer

Flyer starts with one hand on each Bases' shoulder, elbows up. Elbows up will allow Flyer to get a good push off of the Bases. Flyer then places one foot in one of the Base's hands. On count, Flyer will bend the other knee as Bases squat, and push on Bases' shoulders to load other foot into the other Bases' hands (this is referred to as Sponge Position). As Bases drive Flyer upward, Flyer should push off of the Bases' shoulders and lock her legs and tighten up her body as she stands up straight and hits the Prep Position. Flyer should be careful to not sit back or lean forward as Flyer is driven up.

Back Spot

Back Spot will start holding the Flyer's waist and assist her into the Bases' hands. Back Spot and Flyer will squat, and as Flyer jumps, Back Spot will drive Flyer upward. Once the Flyer's feet are in the Bases' hands, the Back Spot will move her hands to the Flyer's ankles and lift upward as the Flyer is driven upward. Back Spot will maintain visual and physical contact with the Back Spot throughout the rest of the stunt, and until the Flyer is safely on the ground.

Half Elevator/Prep

Position
1 Foot load - Technique

Bases' hands are placed at hip level

Base's hand position 1. Front hand grabs under Toe, back hand grabs under heel

Base's hand position 1 (Bottom View)

Base's hand position 2 (Bottom View) Arms are close to chest and under foot

Base's hand position 2 (Front View)

Half Elevator/Prep

1 Foot load - Technique

1. Flyer starts with 1 foot in Base's hand, hands on Base's shoulders. Back Spot has hands on Flyer's ankle

2. View from front

3. Flyer squats and jumps to place other foot in Other Base's hand

4. Bases holding both feet of Flyer. Front view

5. Bases squat

6. As Bases drive Flyer up, **Flyer pushes off** shoulders and stands up

7. Bases begin to change hand postition and drive Flyer to their eye level

8. Rear View

9. Bases lower Flyer to shoulder/Prep level

10. Rear View

11. Flyer finishes stunt - High V

Stunt Explanation

Bases

Bases start facing each other, with legs shoulder width apart and knees bent. Hands are together, palm up (fingertips touching other Base's fingertips). On count, the Flyer will jump in with both feet at the same time. The Bases will squat and drive up to shoulder level. While the Bases are bringing the feet up to shoulder level, they stand up and also switch their grip on the feet. The new grip will be heel & toe – front foot on Flyer's toe and Back hand on Flyer's heel. Bases should get as much of their hands under the Flyers feet as possible. Only the fingertips will wrap the heel and toe. Bases will also keep arms close to their own chests for more support.

Flyer

Flyer starts with one hand on each Bases' shoulder, elbows up. Elbows up will allow Flyer to get a good push off of the Bases. Flyer will squat and jump, and push on Bases' shoulders to be able to place one foot into each of the Bases' hands (this is referred to as a Sponge Position). As Bases drive Flyer upwards Flyer should push off of the Bases' shoulders and lock her legs and tighten up her body as she stands up straight and hits the Prep Position.

Back Spot

Back Spot will start holding the Flyers waist and assist her into the Bases' hands. Once the Flyer's feet are in the Bases' hands, the Back Spot will move her hands to the Flyer's ankles and lift upward as the Flyer is driven upward. Back Spot will maintain visual and physical contact with the Flyer throughout the rest of the stunt, and until the Flyer is safely on the ground.

Half Elevator/Prep

Position
Jump in - 2 Foot Technique

Bases' hands are placed at hip level

Base's hand position 1. Front hand grabs under Toe, back hand grabs under heel

Base's hand position 1 (Bottom View)

Base's hand position 2 (Bottom View)
Arms are close to chest and under foot

Base's hand position 2 (Front View)

Half Elevator/Prep

2 Foot load - Technique

1. Flyer starts with feet together, hands on Base's shoulders. Back Spot has hands on Flyer's ankle

2. Flyer Squats

3. Flyer jumps to place both feet in Base's hands

4. Bases holding both feet of Flyer. Front view

5. Bases squat

6. As Bases drive Flyer up, **Flyer pushes off shoulders and stands up**

7. Bases begin to change hand postition and drive Flyer to their eye level

8. Rear View

9. Bases lower Flyer to shoulder/Prep level

10. Rear View

11. Flyer finishes stunt - High V

57

Half Elevator/Prep

Stunt Explanation

This stunt will start after the stunt group has reached Prep Position on Page 54.

Bases

Bases maintain eye contact with each other and on count, the Bases squat. Bases then drive through their legs, and lift the flyer upward and lock arms out.

Flyer

Flyer starts in Prep Position with hands at sides. On count, as Bases squat, Flyer stays tight, with locked legs, until stunt settles into extension. Flyer must not change their weight and put pressure on their toes or heels. Flyer will then hit an endng position i.e. High V

Back Spot

Back Spot starts with hands on Flyer's ankles. As Bases squat, Back Spot supports ankles and assists in driving Flyer upward. As Flyer settles in, Back Spot maintains physical contact with Flyer's ankles, and visual contact with Flyer's head and hips.

Front Spot

Front Spot in this stunt is optional. If used, the Front Spot starts facing the Flyer, with hands on the front of Flyer's toes. Front Spot helps drive Flyer up and for extra stability in the stunt.

Half Elevator to Extension

1. Start at Prep Level

2. Bases, Back Spot, and optional Front Spot, all squat

3. Bases, Back Spot, & optional Front Spot drive Flyer above their heads

4. Flyer hits ending postion when Bases, Back Spot, and optional Front Spot lock their position

Stunt Explanation

Bases

Bases start facing each other. Flyer will place one foot into Base's hands. Flyer will squat and jump, placing other foot onto Base's other hand. On count, Bases and Back Spot squat and drive Flyer upward 6 to 8 inches above prep position. Bases will then lower Flyer into Prep Position. Bases and Back Spot continuously squat and drive Flyer upward until Bases' arms are locked out at Extension Level.

Flyer

Flyer will start with hands on each Bases' shoulder. On count, Flyer will jump into sponge position, placing a foot into each Bases' hands. Flyer pushes off Bases' shoulders and locks legs to ride up to 6 to 8 inches above Bases shoulder level. Then the Bases lower Flyer to a Prep Position, squat and drive Flyer upward, Flyer stays tight with hands at Flyer's side, up to Extension Level, and then lock out legs.

Back Spot

Back Spot starts with hands on Flyer's waist. Back Spot assists Flyer as she places one foot onto Base's hands. Back Spot assists as Flyer jumps to place other foot onto Base's hand. On count, Back Spot squats with Bases and drives Flyer upward 6 to 8 inches above Prep Position. Once at Prep Level, as Bases squat and drive Flyer to Extension, Back Spot keeps hands on Flyer's ankles and follows Bases, helping to lock out Flyer at Extension.

Pump N Go

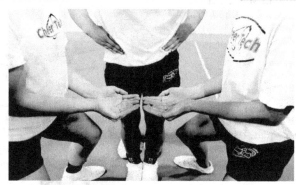

1. Bases hands - Position 1 - at hip level

3. Bases holding both feet of Flyer (Front view)

4. Bases squat

7. Bases lower Flyer to shoulder/ Prep level

8. Bases squat and prepare to drive

Pump N Go

2. Flyer starts with 1 foot in Base's hands, hands on Bases'
shoulders. Back Spot has hands on Flyer's waist

5. Bases begin to drive
(5-10 Shown with Optional Front Spot)

6. As Bases drive Flyer up, Flyer pushes
off Bases' shoulders and stands up

9. Bases drive upward

10. Lock out extension and Flyer
hits end position - High V

Pump N Go

11. Rear view of Half

12. Rear view of squat

13. Rear view of Drive

14. Rear view of Extension

Stunt Explanation

Bases

Bases start facing each other, with legs shoulder width apart and knees bent. Hands are together, palms up (fingertips touching other Base's fingertips). On count, the Flyer will jump in with both feet at the same time. The Bases will squat and drive up to shoulder level. While the Bases are bringing the feet up through shoulder level, they stand up and also switch their grip on the feet. The new grip, Position 2, will be heel & toe – front foot on Flyer's toe and Back hand on Flyer's heel. Bases should get as much of their hands under the Flyer's feet as possible. Only the fingertips will wrap the heel and toe. One Base will continue to drive Flyer's foot upward to extended position. Base will turn forward, pointing Flyer's toe to side. This Base will also lock out arms for more support. Other Base keeps Flyer's foot at prep level, keeping arms in close to chest.

Flyer

Flyer starts with one hand on each Bases' shoulder, elbows up. Elbows up will allow Flyer to get a good push off of the Bases. Flyer will squat and jump, and push on Bases shoulders to be able to place one foot into each of the Bases' hands (this is referred to as a sponge position). As Bases drive Flyer upward, Flyer should push off of the Bases shoulders and lock her legs and tighten up her body as she stands up straight. As Flyer hits the prep position, one of the Flyer's legs will bend at the knee and continue to the extended position. As this happens, the Flyer also transfers her weight to the leg that has stopped at the Prep position. i.e. High V

Back Spot

Back Spot will start holding the Flyer's waist. On count, the Back Spot will help Flyer load in to sponge and drive Flyer upward by throwing waist or grabbing and driving from ankles. Once Flyer passes through Prep Position, the Back Spot will slide hand grip to Flyer's ankle. When one of Flyer's legs is bent and pulled up, Back Spot removes hand from Flyer's ankle and places it on opposite leg of Flyer as high as arm can reach. This is called a splint technique.

Hitch

1. From squat position, Bases drive Flyer up as Flyer pushes off Bases' shoulders

2. Bases and Back Spot continue to drive Flyer up

3. As Flyer drives above Bases eye level, Flyer begins to bend one knee

4. Flyer transfers weight to straight leg as Base drives Hitch leg up. Back Spot grabs under Hitched foot

5. As Flyer Settles in, Hit ending position - High V

6. Splint Technique

This stunt begins in a Sponge Position.

Bases start with hands on Flyer's feet. Right Base will maintain stance and grip while the Left Base squats and drive Flyer's leg upward to extension and turn Left Base's body to face the front. On count, the Right Base will squat and drive Flyer's foot to the top. As the Right Base is driving, the Left Base turns to face the Right Base, stomach, to stomach. Bases must be sure to lock out their arms!

Flyer will keep hips and torso facing forward through stunt. As Flyer squats and drives upward, Flyer will transfer weight to right leg, leaving only 1 to 2 pounds of pressure on the left leg. On count, the Flyer's left leg will be pushed upward to a hitch position. Flyer must bend leg to do this, while remaining tight. On count, as the right Base squats and drives Flyer's right leg to extended position, Flyer must remain tight and lock legs. Once stunt settles in, Flyer will hit ending position.

Back Spot will start with hands on Flyer's ankles as Bases drive through to Prep Position. As Left Base continues driving to extension, Back Spot will release left hand and grab left leg of Flyer in Splint Position for Hitch. As Right Base drives Flyer's Right leg to Extension, Back Spot will re-grab Flyer's left ankle. Back Spot will maintain visual and physical contact with the Flyer throughout the rest of the stunt, and until the Flyer is safely on the ground.

1. From squat position, Bases drive Flyer up as Flyer pushes off Bases' shoulders

4. Flyer transfers weight to straight leg as Base drives Hitch leg up. Back Spot grabs under Hitched foot

7. Straight leg Base squats

64

2. Bases and Back Spot contiue to drive Flyer up

3. As Flyer drives above Bases eye level, Flyer begins to bend one knee

5. As Flyer Settles in, Hit ending position - High V

6. Rear View

8. Base drives Flyer up until legs are even

9. Flyer settles in and hits end postition - High V

Stunt Explanation

This stunt starts in Sponge Position.

Bases

Bases start facing each other, with hand grip in Position 1. On count, Bases squat and drive Flyer upward over the Bases' heads, as high as they can go. When Flyer hits top of ride, Bases immediately begin to lower Flyer to Sponge Position. Bases keep hand grip in Position 1 for the entire stunt.

Flyer

Flyer starts with both feet in Bases' hands and Flyer's hands on Bases' shoulders. On count, Flyer pushes off Bases' shoulders and drives upward straightening legs. At top of ride Flyer hits arm position, in this case High V, and then immediately drops arms. As Bases begin to lower Flyer, the Flyer will place arms on Bases' shoulders to catch Flyer's own weight and return to Sponge Position. It is important for Flyer to keep feet together for entire stunt.

Back Spot

Back Spot starts with hands on Flyer's waist. On count, as Bases drive Flyer upward, Back Spot assists with drives and moves hands to Flyer's ankles. At top of ride and as Flyer is lowered Back Spot maintains physical contact with the Flyer until Flyer is returned to Sponge Position. For more novice Flyer's, Back Spot should hold ankles or Flyer's seat.

Show and Go

1. Flyer starts in Sponge Position

2. Bases start to drive Flyer upward quickly

5. Flyer immediately lowers arms and Bases start to lower Flyer smoothly

3. Bases continue to drive
   Flyer as high as possible

4. Bases hit top, Flyer
   arm position is optional

6. Bases control Flyers descent

7. Flyer returns to
   Sponge Position

Stunt Explanation

Bases

Bases start facing each other, with legs shoulder width apart and knees bent. Hands are together, palms up (fingertips touching other Base's fingertips). On count, the Flyer will load in with either 1 foot or 2 feet technique. The Bases will squat and drive up to extended position. While the Bases are bringing the feet up through shoulder level, they stand up and also switch their grip to Position 2. Bases will also lock arms for more support.

Flyer

Flyer starts with one hand on each Bases' shoulder, elbows up. Elbows up will allow Flyer to get a good push off of the Bases. Flyer will squat and load in with either 1 foot or 2 feet. As Bases drive Flyer upward, Flyer should push off of the Bases' shoulders, lock legs and tighten as Flyer stands up straight and hits the extended position. As Flyer settles in, Flyer hits ending position – High V.

Back Spot

Back Spot will start holding the Flyer's waist and assist the Flyer into the Bases' hands. Once the Flyer's feet are in the Bases hands, the Back Spot will move hands to the Flyer's ankles and lift upward as the Flyer is driven upward. If, as the Flyer goes overhead, the Flyer's ankles are too high, the Back Spot may hold onto the wrists of the Bases. Back Spot will maintain visual and physical contact with the Flyer throughout the rest of the stunt, and until the Flyer is safely on the ground.

Quick Up Extension

Positions

1. Bases hands - Position 1 - at hip level

2. Flyer starts with 1 foot in Base's hand, hands on Bases' shoulders. Back Spot has hands on Flyer's waist

3. Base hands - Position 2 - with optional Front Spot

Quick Up Extension
Technique

1. Bases holding both feet of Flyer   (Front view)

2. Bases squat

3. As Bases drive Flyer up, Flyer pushes off Bases' shoulders and stands up

4. Bases drive upward

5. Lock out extension and Flyer hits end position - High V

Stunt Explanation

Bases

Bases start facing each other, with legs shoulder width apart, knees bent. Hands are together palm up and fingertips touching other Base's fingertips. On count, the Flyer will load in with either 1 foot or 2 feet technique. The Bases will squat and drive up to extended position. While the Bases are bringing the feet up through shoulder level, they stand up and also switch their grip to Position 2. Bases should also stand close together so Flyer's feet are together when locking out arms for more support.

Flyer

Flyer starts with one hand on each of Base's shoulders, elbows up. Elbows up will allow Flyer to get a good push off of the Bases. Flyer will squat and load in with either 1 foot or 2 feet. As Bases drive Flyer upward Flyer pushes off of the Base's shoulders, locking legs and pulls feet together. As Flyer stands up straight, the Bases keep Flyer's legs close together to hit the extended position. As Flyer settles in Flyer hits ending position – High V

Back Spot

Back Spot will start holding the Flyer's waist and assist the Flyer into the Bases' hands. Once the Flyer's feet are in, Back Spot moves hands to the Flyer's ankles as the Flyer is driven upward., and assist Flyer in pulling feet together. Back Spot will maintain visual and physical contact with the Flyer throughout the rest of the stunt, and until the Flyer is safely on the ground.

Quick Up Cupie

1. Flyer starts in Sponge Position, Bases squat

2. Bases drive upward as Flyer pushes off Bases' shoulders

3. Bases drive upward, Flyer stands up

4. Lock out extension and Flyer hits end position - Cupie

70

Stunt Explanation

Bases

Bases start facing each other, with the Flyer on the opposite side – facing the back. The Flyer has hands on both Bases' shoulders and with Right foot in set position. Right Base's hand grip is as follows: Right hand grabs the Flyer's right toe. The left hand will cross over the right hand and grab's Flyers right heel. Left Base's hand grip is as follows: Right hand grabs the Flyer's left toe. The left hand will cross over the right hand and grab Flyer's left heel. On count the Bases and Flyer squat and Flyer jumps, placing left foot into left Base. As the Bases drive upward the Flyer will twist counter clockwise and Bases will continue driving above their heads and settle into half elevator.

Flyer

Flyer starts in front of stunt, facing back wall, with hands on shoulders of Bases. Flyer places right foot in right Base's hands, crossing legs. On count Flyer will jump and place left leg behind right leg to Left Base. (Note: It is important to cross legs this way or Flyer's legs will tangle). As Flyer jumps in, Flyer keeps all weight in arms. As Bases drive upward, Flyer pushes off shoulders and begins to turn counter clockwise 180 degrees. It is important the Flyer keeps legs locked while riding upwards to complete the turn to settle into prep position hitting end position – High V

Back Spot

Back Spot grabs the shins of the Flyer as Flyer loads. As Bases squat and drive, and as Flyer twists, Back Spot grabs Flyer's ankles as high as possible and settle into prep position. Back Spot will maintain visual and physical contact with the Back Spot throughout the rest of the stunt, and until the Flyer is safely on the ground.

Half Twist In

Positions

1. Left Base - Position 1
 White Glove - under heel - Left hand
 Black Glove - under toe - Right hand

2. Left Base
Underneath view

3. Right Base - Position 1
White Glove - under heel - Right hand
Black Glove - under toe - Left Hand

4. Both Bases - Position 1
Underneath view

5. Left Base - Position 2

6. Right Base - Position 2

Half Twist In

Technique

1. Flyer places Right foot in Right Base's Hands

2. Flyer jumps in as Bases squat, placing Left foot in Left Base's hands

3. Flyer shrugs as Bases begin to drive Flyer upwards

4. Flyer rides and turns counterclockwise

5. Flyer stops rotation at prep level

6. Flyer hits stunt

Stunt Explanation

Start this stunt from prep position on page 54.

Bases

Bases have Flyer's feet in hands and on count, Bases and Back Spot squat, drive about 6 inches above their heads to change hand positions to position 1. Bases then bring Flyer back to sponge position, bounce and drive Flyer back up above head, change hands to position 2, and settle in at prep position.

Flyer

Flyer starts in prep position with hands at side. As Bases squat, Flyer remains tight, and starts to bend knees and put weight to Bases shoulders through Flyer's hands, when Flyer settles to sponge position. Bases will begin to drive Flyer upward, as Flyers pushes through arms keeping body tight, locking legs out, and pulling feet together as Flyer rides up to Prep Position.

Back Spot

Back Spot starts with hands on ankles. On count, Back Spot squats, continuing to hold ankles, drives upward, and settles to sponge position. On bounce, the Back Spot assists in the drive above the Base's heads and settles back in prep position.

Note: For young/inexperienced stunt groups Back Spot can grab upper thighs or waist of Flyer for additional support.

Double Take

Positions

1. Hand Position 1

2. Prep Hand Position 2
Option A - No Front Spot

3. Prep Hand Position 2
Option B - Front Spot

4. Drive Hand Position 1
Option A - No Front Spot

5. Drive Hand Position 2
Option B - Front Spot

6. Squat Hand Position 1
Option B - Front Spot

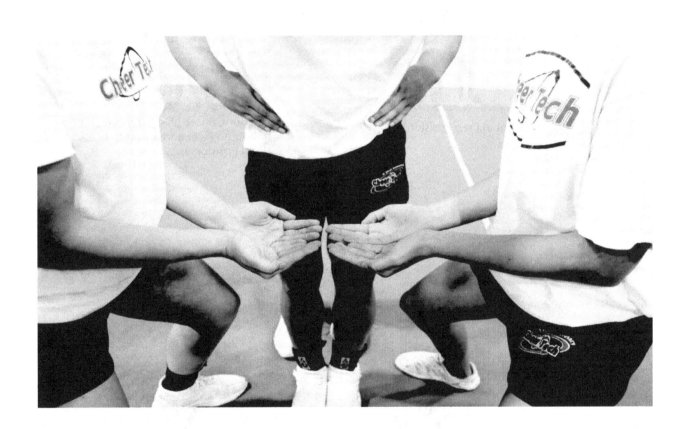

1. Set in Prep Position

2. On count, Bases give baby pop to lighten Flyer and adjust to Hand Position 1

5. Hit Squat position and bounce up

6. Drive Flyer upward

3. Bring Flyer down to Squat position

4. Flyer places arms on Base's shoulders

7. Drive upwards through Prep Position

8. Settle in at Prep Position

Stunt Explanation

This stunt starts from Extension Position on page 59.

Bases

Bases have Flyer's feet in hands and on count, Bases and Back Spot squat and baby pop, driving Flyer upward to change hand positions to position 1. Bases then bring Flyer to sponge position and bounce and drive Flyer back up above head, change hands to position 2, and lock arms out at extension.

Flyer

Flyer starts in Extension Position. On count, as Bases squat, Flyer remains tight, and starts to bend knees and put weight onto Bases' shoulders through Flyer's hands, when Flyer settles to sponge position. Bases will begin to drive Flyer upward, as Flyer pushes through arms keeping body tight and locking legs out as Flyer rides up to extension position.

Back Spot

Back Spot starts with hands on ankles. On count, Back Spot squats, continuing to hold ankles, drives upward and settles to sponge position. On bounce, the Back Spot assists in the drive above the Base's heads and settles back in extension position.

Note: For more novice Flyers, Back Spot can release ankles and grab Flyer's upper legs (hamstring or seat) and drive Flyer back up, grabbing ankles to stabilize.

Double Take Extension

1. Flyer starts in Extension

2. Bases squat for Baby pop to change hand position

5. Flyer supports weight on Bases' shoulders. Bases squat and prepare to drive Flyer upward

6. Bases drive Flyer upward

Double Take Extension

3. Bases begin to lower Flyer. Back Spot releases ankles and reaches for Flyer

4. Flyer settles into Sponge Position

7. Flyer locks legs out and stands up as Bases continue to drive

8. Flyer hits stunt

Stunt Explanation

Stunt can begin from the basket position page 156 or with a prep position Page 54. Both are acceptable.

Bases

Bases will maintain grip on heel and toe of Flyer, Position 2, throughout the stunt. On count, Bases will follow feet of Flyer as she is guided into the 'basket'. On count, Bases will squat and drive their arms and Flyer straight to extension. Be sure to lock out arms to maintain a steady surface for Flyer.

Flyer

Flyer will bend and keep knees together as she is lowered to the basket. As Flyer lands in basket, Flyer places arms on Basket Base's shoulders. As Basket Bases squat, Flyer pushes off of the Basket Base's shoulders and stands up into the extension position. The Flyer then settles into the stunt and hits end position

Basket Bases

Basket Bases stand in front of and shoulder to shoulder with Bases. Hand grip is: Left Basket Base has Right hand on Left wrist and Left hand on Right Basket Base's Right hand. Right Basket Base has Right hand on Left wrist and Left hand on Left Basket Base's Right wrist. As Flyer puts knees together and bends forward, Basket Bases raise arms to catch Flyer. Basket Bases then lower hands and squat, beginning to drive Flyer back upward by pushing through Basket Grip.

Back Spot

Back Spot holds onto Flyer's ankles and on count, guides the Flyer to her knees in the Basket that the Basket Bases have formed. On count, Back Spot will guide the Flyer's ankles and help pull Flyer to Extension. Back Spot maintains eye contact on Flyer during entire stunt to maintain stability and safety.

Knee Drop
Positions

1. Basket Bases grip position

2. Basket held high for catch

3. Flyer uses arms on Basket Bases' shoulders to take weight off Basket Bases

4. Basket Bases squat for toss

Knee Drop

Technique

1. Set Position

2. Flyer bends knees and starts to fall into Basket

3. Bases catch and squat

4. Bases toss back up

5. Hit Extension

Stunt Explanation

This stunt starts in a prep position as on page 54.

Bases

Bases start with hands in position 2 under Flyer's feet. On count, Right Base will squat and drive Flyer's right leg upward, while releasing left hand from Flyer's right foot and grabbing Flyer's upper thigh with Right Base's Left hand. At the same time, Right Base will turn forward to face the crowd. On the same count, Left Base will squat and drive Flyer's left leg upward, while releasing right hand from Flyer's left foot and grabbing Flyer's upper thigh with Left Base's right hand. At the same time, Left Base will turn backwards away from the crowd. On count, Both Bases will squat and drive Flyer upward, pushing up on Flyer's inner thighs and pulling Flyer's feet underneath Flyer and up above Bases' heads. Bases will then let go of Flyer's upper thighs and grab the Flyer's feet and settle into Prep position.

Flyer

Flyer starts in prep position and will prepare for Right Split. On count, the Flyer reaches and grabs the hands of the Front Pole, for balance and control. On count, as the Bases squat and drive, Flyer does a right split supporting body weight on the arms of the Front Pole. The Bases will then drive Flyer's feet together and up, back into Prep position. Flyer will settle into position, release hands of front pole and hit end position at prep.

Front Pole

Front Pole stands in front of stunt facing flyer and on count, will grab Flyer's hands keeping arms locked and in close to Front Pole's ears. As Flyer descends into split, Front Pole may bend arms to help support Flyer's weight and keep control of Flyer into and out of stunt. Front Pole will them help drive Flyer upward into prep position by allowing Flyer to press down on Front Poles arms. Front Pole will then release arms and maintain visual contact with Flyer.

Back Spot

Back Spot will start with hands on Flyer's ankles. On count, Back Spot will squat and drive Flyer upward and release Flyer's ankles to grab Flyer's upper inner thighs of both legs to help stabilize split. Back Spot will then drive Flyer's inner thighs upward, to Prep position, releasing inner thighs and grabbing Flyer's ankles. Back Spot will maintain visual contact with Flyer.

Half Split Half

1. Flyer starts in a prep position

4. Bases let go of Flyer's feet with inside hand and grab Flyer's inner thigh

7. Flyer hits split and Bases squat

82

2. Flyer grabs Front Spot's hands as Bases squat

3. Bases pop Flyer upward

5. Flyer pivots hips to go into right split

6. Bases turn to face Flyer's leg and support Flyer's right split

8. Bases drive Flyer upward

9. Flyer pulls legs together. Bases release Flyer's legs and regrip Flyer's feet

10. Flyer returns to prep position

Stunt Explanation

Bases
Bases start with hands, palms up, on the ground to let Flyer step in. Flyer carefully stands on Bases' hands, and Bases grip Flyer's feet. On count, Flyer jumps to allow Bases to drive Flyer straight up to extension, changing grip to position 2 during drive. Bases must lock out arms at top of drive.

Flyer
Flyer starts in front of Back Spot. Flyer places feet ever so lightly on Bases' hands, first right then left foot. On count, Flyer squats and jumps, driving upward, locking legs out as Flyer pushes off Bases' shoulders. Flyer remains tight as Flyer drives to extension.

Back Spot
Back Spot starts holding waist of Flyer. On count, Back Spot squats and drives Flyer upward, releasing Flyer and re-grabbing Flyer's ankles continuing to drive Flyer upward to extension. Option: Back Spot can start holding Flyer's ankles, and when Flyer jumps, drive Flyer upward from ankles straight up to extension.

1. Bases place hands on floor, palms up. Flyer places left foot on Bases' hand ever so lightly

2. Flyer places other foot on Bases' hand, again very lightly

5. As Flyer jumps up, Bases begin to drive Flyer upward

6. Bases continue to drive as Flyer stays tight

Ground Up Extension

3. Flyer starts to squat

4. Flyer begins to jump

7. Bases change hand grip to
   Position 2 and Bases continue to drive

8. Flyer hits stunt

Stunt Explanation

This stunt starts from prep position as on page 54.

Bases

Bases start holding Flyer's feet. On count, Bases squat and drive Flyer up and forward through Front Pole's arms, releasing Flyer's feet. Bases then walk forward, following stunt, and catching Flyer's feet as high as possible, bringing Flyer back down to prep position(or to sponge position – optional).

Flyer

Flyer starts at prep position. Flyer will reach forward and grab the arms of Front Pole. On count, as the Bases drive Flyer upward, the Flyer will push down through Front Pole's arms and pull up into a tuck position, enabling the Flyer to go over the head of the Front Pole. Flyer will keep as much weight in the arms of the pole as long as possible to ensure the Bases can get a good grip on Flyer's feet. As the Bases re-grab Flyer's feet, the Flyer will lock legs and stand up in prep position.

Front Pole

Front Pole stands in front of the Flyer with arms above head, locked out, keeping biceps by ears. On count, as Bases drive Flyer upward, Flyer will push down on Front Pole's arms. It is important that Front Pole keeps arms locked to prevent getting kicked and to keep the Flyer stable and safe. As the Flyer goes overhead and lands in the Base's hands, the Front Pole now becomes the Back Spot of the stunt. Front Pole will release Flyer's hands and grab Flyer's hamstrings.

Back Spot

Back Spot will start with hands on Flyer's ankles. As Bases squat, Back Spot will help drive Flyer up and forward releasing ankles when Flyer is supported by Front Pole.

Note: If using only 4 people in stunt group, which would be for the more advanced, it is strongly recommend that the Back Spot walks around stunt to Front Pole Position and DOES NOT walk under the Flyer. Best recommendation is to have 5 in group for safety.

Leap Frog

1. Flyer reaches for Front Pole

2. Bases start squat to thrust Flyer upwards

5. Bases follow Flyer and catch feet

6. Bases take Flyer to squat position

Leap Frog

Technique

3. Flyer rides up into tuck position

4. Flyer goes through the arms of Front Pole

7. Base Drive Flyer upwards

8. Stunt settles at prep position

BEGINNER & INTERMEDIATE STUNTS

STUNTING 3

Stunt Explanation

This stunt starts in a cradle on page 150.

Bases

Bases start by holding Flyer's back and legs in a cradle. On count, Bases squat and drive Flyer upward, catching Flyer at Prep Level. Bases will grab under Flyer's mid/low back and upper hamstrings.

Flyer

Flyer starts in cradle position. On count, as Bases drive Flyer upward, Flyer must pull up hips into a straight body position and stay extremely tight. Once in Flat Back Position, other positions are acceptable.

Back Spot

Back Spot starts supporting Flyer's armpits. On count, Back Spot squats and drives Flyer upward, catching Flyer at prep level with hands under Flyer's shoulders.

Note: If extending Flat Back Position to extension, make sure Bases and Back Spot completely lock out arms and spread out hand placement to evenly distribute Flyer's weight. Keep eyes on Flyer at all times.

1. Flyer starts in a cradle

4. Bases snap arms to release Flyer

7. Bases drive Flyer upward to Extended Flatback

Flatback

2. Bases squat

3. Bases drive Flyer upward

5. Flyer hits Flatback

6. Bases squat

8. Side View of squat

9. Side View of Flatback

10. Side view of Extended Flatback

Stunt Explanation

Bases

Base stands in front of Flyer and squats. Flyer reaches behind keeping arms by ears, bent at elbows, and grabs armpits of Flyer. On count, Base will squat and lock Base's arms, keeping arms close to Base's ears and supporting Flyer by armpits.

Flyer

Flyer starts by standing behind Base, with hands on Base's shoulders and Base's hands under Flyer's armpits. On count, Flyer will squat and jump upward, pushing through the shoulders of the Base. As Base locks arms, Flyer will pull legs up into a toe touch position so that Flyer can grab Flyer's ankles to lock stunt out.

Back Spot

Back Spot starts standing behind Flyer and holding Flyer's waist. On count, Base will squat and lift Flyer up for stability and safety supporting Flyer's waist for duration of stunt.

On count, Base squats and pops Flyer backward releasing Flyer's armpits. Flyer releases ankles and closes legs bending knees as Flyer returns to ground.. Back Spot maintains contact with Flyer's waist returning Flyer to ground.

Star

1. Base squats, grabs armpits of Flyer

2. Base locks arms out as Flyer jumps up and lifts legs into Toe Touch

3. Flyer grabs ankles and hits Star

Stunt Explanation

Bases

Bases start with Flyer in cradle position with Flyer's hands on Bases' shoulders. On count, Bases squat and pop flyer straight upward, allowing Flyer to twist 360 degrees above Bases' heads. Bases should keep arms up after release to catch Flyer high. Bases will then catch Flyer in cradle position.

1. Flyer starts in cradle

2. Bases squat

Flyer

Flyer starts in cradle position with arms around Bases' shoulders. On count, as Bases squat, Flyer is popped and Flyer will ride upwards twisting 360 degrees to the left, keeping feet together. Flyer will then return to slight V position and catch Bases' shoulder in cradle position.

Back Spot

Back Spot starts holding Flyer's shoulders. On count, Back Spot squats with Bases and helps drive Flyer upward. Back Spot also is in control of Flyer to help make sure Flyer doesn't twist early enabling Flyer to go up and down in same position. As Flyer lands, Back Spot controls landing by re-grabbing under Flyer's shoulders.

5. Flyer continues rotation

6. As Flyer finishes rotation, Bases prepare to catch Flyer

3. Bases drive Flyer upwards,
   and Flyer rotates

4. Flyer continues rotation

7. Flyer returns to a cradle

Stunt Explanation

Bases

Right Base will be on Flyer's right hand side and grabs the Flyer's right ankle with Base's right hand. Base's left hand will go under the upper thigh of the Flyer. On count, Flyer will squat and jump. Right Base will drive Flyer up to Shoulder height.

Left Base will catch Flyer's left leg, the Leg that the Flyer lifts after jumping. Left Base will grab Flyer's left ankle with left hand. Base's right hand goes under Flyer's upper thigh.

Flyer

Flyer puts hands on shoulders of Both Bases. Flyer lifts right leg parallel to the floor so Right Base can grab right leg. On count, Flyer will squat and jump, pushing off shoulders of Bases and lifting left leg into straddle position. Flyer must also crunch stomach muscles to sit in straddle position on Base's hands.

Back Spot

Back Spot holds waist of Flyer. On count, as Flyer squats and jumps, Back Spot throws up from waist of Flyer and support Flyer's seat at shoulder level.

Dismount

On count, Bases will close Flyer's legs and drop Flyer through to cradle. Back Spot will catch under armpits and help support cradle.

Option

This stunt can also be preformed to extended level, where Bases lock out arms above head. Back Spot MUST maintain visual contact with Flyer. Note: certain rules may require an additional Back Spot.

1. Flyer places hands on Bases' shoulders. Back spot holds Flyers waist. One base holds ankle of Flyer and under upper thigh

2. On count, Flyer jumps. Base 2 comes in and grabs other leg under upper thigh and ankle

4. On count, Bases can squat and drive to Extended level. An extra spotter maybe required

96

Straddle Sit

3. Back Spot moves hands under
   Flyer's seat. Flyer sits up straight and
   places hands on hips

5. Dismount - Bases press Flyer's feet together

6. Bases drop her into cradle

Straddle Sit

Stunt Explanation

Straddle Sit to Prep

This stunt starts with a Straddle Sit as seen on page 96.

Bases
Bases will start by putting their outside hand on the bottom side of Flyer's toe. Bases' inside hand will remain underneath the Flyer's upper thigh. The Bases' outside hand will move to the Flyer's toe. On count, Bases will squat and drive the Flyer's legs upward to the prep position. As the Bases drive their inside hand up, they also step in toward the other Base. In addition, the Base's inside hand moves to Flyer's heel.

Flyer
Flyer starts in a straddle position. As the Bases squat and drive, the Flyer squeezes thighs together and stand up in Prep Position, staying tight.

Back Spot
Back Spot starts with hands under Flyer's seat. On count, as Bases squat, Back Spot also squats and drives Flyer to prep position. As the Flyer goes from a sitting to a standing position, the Back Spot's hands move to Flyer's ankles and maintain physical and visual contact throughout the stunt.

1. Flyer places hands on Bases' shoulders. Back spot holds Flyer's waist. One Base holds ankle of Flyer and under upper thigh

2. On count, Flyer jumps and raises other leg. Back spot and Bases drive Flyer up

3. Base 2 grabs Flyer's Leg, one hand under ankle other hand under upper thigh

4. Back spot moves hands under Flyer's seat. Flyer places hands on Hips

5. Bases squat and drive inside hand up. Back Spot drives Flyer up

6. Back Spot grabs Flyer's ankles, Bases move inside hand to under Flyers feet

99

Stunt Explanation

This stunt begins with shoulder sit as on Page 32.

In this stunt the Back Spot actually starts the stunt as the Base, and will be referred to as Back Spot. In this stunt an additional Back Spot was used for safety.

Bases

Bases stand in front of Back Spot and grab Flyer's feet under toe and heel with fingertips facing the other Base. On count, Bases and Back Spot squat and pop the Flyer using the power from their legs to help Flyer stand upright and off the shoulders of the Back Spot. Bases then continue to drive Flyer upward into Prep Position.

Flyer

Flyer starts by sitting on Back Spot's shoulders, and placing a foot into each Base's hands. As Bases and Back Spot squat, Flyer places hands on the Bases' shoulders and push off Base's own thighs on count. Flyer will squeeze and lock legs out. At the top, Flyer will hit a high ending position - High V

Back Spot

Back Spot starts with Flyer on shoulders and hands underneath Flyer's thighs. On count, Bases and Back Spot squat and drive Flyer's upper thighs upwards, pushing Flyer off shoulders into Prep Position and grabbing ankles of Flyer. As soon as Flyer's drive starts to leave Base's shoulders, Back Spot's eyes should be on Flyer.

Shoulder Sit to Prep
Rear View

1. Start stunt in Shoulder Sit. Back Spot squats

2. Back Spot drives with hands under Flyers hamstrings. Bases squat and drive Flyer up

3. Back Spot grabs ankles and continue to drive Flyer up with Bases

4. Bases return Flyer to Prep Level. Flyer hits End Position - High V

Shoulder Sit to Prep

Front View

1. Start in Shoulder Sit. Flyer has hands on Bases' Shoulders.

2. Bases and Back Spot squat

3. Flyer pushes off Bases' shoulders and stands up.

4. Back Spot grabs ankles and drives Flyer up with help from Bases.

5. Bases and Back Spot return Flyer to Prep Level. Flyer Hits End Position - High V

Stunt Explanation

Bases

Base will stand facing crowd. Flyer does handstand about 2 feet behind Base. Flyer bends at knees and drops legs onto Base's shoulder. Base squats and holds Flyer's shins tightly. Base will pull down on Flyer's shins as Flyer curls up into Shoulder Sit, remaining in squat position until Flyer is upright. Base then stands upright.

Flyer

Flyer starts about 3 feet behind Base and does a handstand about 2 feet from Base. Flyer will bend knees and hook legs onto Base's shoulders. When Base grabs Flyer's shins, Flyer curls up, as in a situp, to a seated position on Base's shoulders. For best support, the Flyer squeezes her legs and top of shoelaces into Base's kidneys once in Shoulder Sit.

Back Spot

Back Spot is the most important position in this stunt. When Flyer is in the handstand, Back Spot must control the Flyer and help align the Flyer's legs as Flyer bends knees onto Base's shoulders. Back Spot then assists Flyer in curl up to Shoulder Sit Position on Base's shoulders.

1. Base squats, Back Spot prepares to catch Flyer

4. Back Spot grabs Flyer's waist for support

7. Flyer curls up to sit position

Handstand to Shoulder Sit

2. Flyer starts handstand

3. Back Spot prepares to catch Flyer

5. Flyer hits handstand position, Base prepares to catch ankles

6. Base grabs Flyer's ankles

8. Back Spot assists Flyer in sitting up

9. Flyer hits stunt

10. Front View

Stunt Explanation

This stunt starts in Prep Position on page_____

Bases

Bases start with hands on Flyer's feet in Sponge Position. On count, Bases squat and drive Flyer upward. At top of drive, Bases will release Flyer, allowing Flyer to rotate forward. Bases will keep arms extended with palms up to catch Flyer in cradle position. Bases are responsible for catching and supporting Flyer's back and legs, over-compensating for Back Spot.

Flyer

Flyer starts in Sponge Position with hands behind Flyer, grabbing the hands of the Back Spot. On count, Flyer will ride upward and execute a forward roll when released from Bases and while staying connected to Back Spot. Flyer will end in a "V" cradle position, releasing grip with Back Spot once in cradle.

Back Spot

Back Spot releases Flyer's ankles and grabs hands with Flyer. On count Bases drive Flyer upward while Back Spot locks arms so Flyer can get maximum height to execute forward roll. Keeping arms locked is important for safety and appearance. Back Spot must stay connected with Flyer until Flyer is safely in cradle position.

Front Spot

Front Spot in this stunt is optional. Front Spots will assist with drive of Flyer, releasing Flyer at top of drive. Front Spot also will assist on catching Flyer in cradle.

Suspended Roll

1. Flyer sets, grip with Back Spot

2. Flyer and Bases squat

5. Bases release feet

6. Flyer continues rotating

9. Bases absorb cradle

10. Bases and Flyer in Cradle

Suspended Roll

3. Bases and Back Spot drive Flyer

4. Flyer starts roll. Back Spot extends arms and maintains contact with Flyer

7. Bases keep hands up as Flyer continues to roll

8. Bases catch Flyer high, Back Spot still has Flyer's hands

11. Rear View - Hand grip

12. Side View - Hand grip

ONE LEG STUNTS

4

STUNTING

Prep Positions

1. Dead Leg

2. Liberty

3. Heel Stretch

4. Arabesque

5. Scale

6. Bow and Arrow

7. Power Stretch

8. Scorpion

Extended Positions

1. Liberty

2. Heel Stretch

3. Arabesque

4. Scorpion

5. Cupie/Awesome

Positions and Techniques

Bow and Arrow

A. Start with Heel Stretch

B. Pull Arm Through

C. Straighten Arm

Scale

A. Grab shin from Behind

B. Extend Leg

Power Stretch

A. Start with Heel Stretch

B. Pull Arm Through

C. Straighten Arm

D. Place arm on elbow and release other hand

Liberty Hand Positions Bases only

Right Base

Right hand holds the front Toe of the Flyer (Black Glove in Picture 2)

Left hand holds the heel of the Flyer. (White Glove in Picture 2)

Left Base

Right hand holds the bottom of the Flyer's foot inbetween the Right base's hands (White Glove in Picture 3)

Left hand holds the top of the Flyer's foot, locking the foot of the Flyer as tight as possible. (Black Glove in Picture 4)

1. Liberty   2. Right base - Black Glove is Right Hand, Front Toe - White Glove is Left Hand, Heel

3. Left Base - White Glove is Right Hand Under Foot and Inbetween Right Base's Hands

4. Left Base - Black Glove is Left Hand, Supports top of Flyer's Foot. Lock Foot of Flyer as Tight as Possible

Liberty

Stunt Explanation

Bases

Bases stand facing each other. Right Base will grab under Flyer's right foot, under the toe, with right hand and Flyer's heel with left hand.

Left Base will grab under Flyer's foot with right hand between Right Base's hands, and left hand on top of Flyer's Foot, clamping down on Flyer's foot as tight as possible. On count, Bases squat and drive Flyer upward to an extended 1 legged position. As Bases drive upward they must also step in as close as possible to one another and lock elbows out.

Flyer

Flyer will place right foot into Base's hands, and both hands on the shoulder of both Bases. On count, Flyer will squat with Bases and drive through arms to lock out Flyer's right leg continuing up to extended level. As Flyer is about to settle into stunt the Flyer lifts and bends the free leg to her knee to Liberty position.

Note: Other 1 legged stunts can be executed from this stunt.

Back Spot

Back Spot has right hand on Flyer's right ankle and left hand under Flyer's seat. On count, the Back Spot squats with Bases and Flyer, and drives the seat of the Flyer as fast as possible to help Flyer lock the right leg out. As the Back Spot drives Flyer upward, move the left hand to the Flyer's right ankle for extra power and support.

Press Up Liberty

1. Right base - Black Glove is Right Hand, Front Toe - White Glove is Left Hand, Heel

2. Left Base - White Glove is Right Hand Under Foot Between Right Base's Hands

3. Left Base - Black Glove is Left Hand, Supports top of Flyer's Foot. Lock Foot of Flyer as Tight as Possible

114

Press Up Liberty

1. On count Flyer and Bases squat

2. Bases drive Flyer upwards toward ceiling

3. Bases arms should lock out

4. Flyer executes trick, Liberty

Stunt Explanation

Bases

Bases stand facing each other. Flyer will line up a few feet behind Bases. On count, Flyer walks forward and steps into Bases' hands with Flyer's Right foot. Right Base will grab under Flyer's right foot, under the toe, with right hand and Flyer's heel with left hand.

Left Base will grab under Flyer's right foot with right hand between Right Base's hands, and left hand on top of Flyer's Foot, clamping down on Flyer's foot as tight as possible. As Flyer steps into the Bases, the Bases will squat, and drive Flyer upward through to an extended 1 legged position. As Bases drive upward, they must also step in as close as possible to one another and lock elbows out.

Flyer

Flyer will line up 2-3 feet behind Bases. Flyer steps forward with left foot and steps into the Bases' hands with the right foot. Flyer also places Flyer's hands onto each Bases' shoulder. As Flyer steps in, Flyer will squat with Bases, and drive through arms to lock out Flyer's right leg while continuing up to extended level. As Flyer is about to settle into the stunt, the Flyer lifts and bends the free leg to hit Liberty position.

Back Spot

Back Spot will stand shoulder to shoulder with the Right Base. As Flyer walks into the stunt, the Back Spot will follow Flyer in and grab the Flyer's ankle with right hand and the Flyer's seat with left hand. Back Spot will squat as Bases and Flyer squat and drive the seat of the Flyer as fast as possible, until the Flyer locks the right leg out. As the Back Spot continues to drive, the left hand will move to Flyer's right ankle for extra power and support.

Walk Up Liberty

Positions

1. Right Base - Black Glove is Right Hand, Front Toe - White Glove is Left Hand, Heel

2. Left Base - White Glove is Right Hand On Foot Between Right Base's Hands

3. Left Base - Black Glove is Left Hand, Supports top of Flyer's Foot. Lock Foot of Flyer as Tight as Possible

4. Back Spot View

116

Walk Up Liberty

Technique

1. Flyer steps with Left Leg

2. Step in with Right Leg. Back Spot starts to swoop in

3. Bases grip foot and start to dip

4. Back Spot gets Right hand to Right Ankle and Left hand on Flyer's seat

5. Group Squats

6. Drives through to top

7. Back Spot helps lock out stunt

Stunt Explanation

Bases

Bases stand facing each other. Flyer will line up a few feet behind Bases. On count, Flyer walks forward and steps into Base's hands. Right Base will grab under Flyer's right foot, under the toe with right hand and Flyer's heel with left hand.

Left Base will grab under Flyer's foot with right hand between Right Base's hands, and left hand on top of Flyer's Foot, clamping down on Flyer's foot as tight as possible. As Flyer steps into the Bases, the Bases will squat and drive Flyer upward 6 - 8 inches above Bases head and down to prep level. As the Flyer hits prep level, the Bases squat and drive the Flyer upward, this time to extension level. As Bases drive upward, they must also step in as close as possible to one another and lock elbows out.

Flyer

Flyer will place right foot into Base's hands, and both hands on the shoulder of both Bases. On count, Flyer will squat with Bases and drive through arms to lock out Flyer's right leg. Flyer will then ride above prep level and return to prep level. As Bases squat again, Flyer remains tight and locked as Flyer goes to an Extended Position, and bends free leg to hit Liberty Position.

Back Spot

Back Spot has right hand on Flyer's right ankle and left hand under Flyer's seat. On count, the Back Spot squats with Bases and Flyer, and drives the seat of the flyer as fast as possible to help Flyer lock the right leg out. Back Spot will squat with the Bases and again drive Flyer to Extended Position. As the Back Spot drives Flyer upward, move the left hand to the Flyer's right ankle for extra power and support.

Front Spot

Front Spot in this stunt is optional. Front Spots will assist with drive of Flyer to Prep Position, and again to Extended Position.

Pump N Go Liberty

Positions

1. Right Base - Black Glove is Right Hand, Front Toe
   White Glove is Left Hand, Heel

2. Left Base - White Glove is Right Hand
   On Foot Between Right Base's Hands

3. Left Base - Black Glove is Left Hand, Supports top of Flyer's Foot.
   Lock Foot of Flyer as tight as Possible

4. One leg grip with help of optional Front Spot

118

1. On count, group squats

2. Bases drive Flyer above Prep Position

3. Bases squat at Prep Position,
   Flyer's Leg pulled up at this point is Optional

4. Bases drive Flyer up to Extension
   Flyer pulls leg up and hits stunt

5. Back spot view

Stunt Explanation

Bases

Bases stand facing each other. Right Base will grab under Flyer's right foot, under the toe with right hand and Flyer's heel with left hand. Left Base will grab under Flyer's foot with right hand between Right Base's hands, and left hand on top of Flyer's Foot, clamping down on Flyer's foot as tight as possible. On count, Bases squat and drive Flyer upward to 6 inches above Base's head. As Bases hit Prep Position, the Bases squat and drive Flyer upward again to an extended 1 leg position. As Bases drive upward, they must also step in as close as possible to one another and lock elbows out.

Flyer

Flyer will place right foot into Base's hands, and both hands on the shoulder of both Bases. On count, Flyer will squat with Bases and drive through arms to lock out Flyer's right leg, continuing up to 6 inches above Bases' heads and hit prep position. As Bases squat again Flyer steps with Left leg to the front of the stunt to front spots hands. Flyer keeps most of weight on Flyer's right leg. As Bases drive Flyer upwards, Front Spot drives Flyer's left leg upward and Flyer bends left leg to knee to Liberty Position. Flyer will settle into stunt and hit ending position

Back Spot

Back Spot's right hand is on Flyer's right ankle and Back Spot's left hand is under Flyer's seat. On count, Back Spot squats with Bases and drives Flyer's seat upward as fast as possible to enable Flyer's right leg to lock out. As Back Spot is driving Flyer upward, Back Spots left hand leaves Flyer's seat and grabs Flyer's right ankle for extra power and support. Back Spot's hands remain on Flyer's right ankle as Bases and Back Spot squat and drive Flyer's ankle upward into extension.

Front Spot

Front Spot starts in front of stunt. When Flyer is driven up to Prep Position, Front Spot extends arms so Flyer can step onto Front Spot's hands with Flyer's left foot. Front Spot squats with Bases and when Bases drive Flyer upward, Front Spot drives and releases Flyer's foot. Front Spot remains in front of stunt for stability and safety.

1. Base sets grip, and squats

2. Flyer and Base drive

3. Flyer is at Prep Position, Flyer sets Trigger on Front Spot

4. Bases squat

5. Front spot throws foot, Bases drive up to extension

6. Flyer pulls leg up to hit Liberty

120

Stunt Explanation

Start this stunt from Liberty position page 112.

Bases

Bases have Flyer's right foot in Liberty position. On count, Bases and Back Spot squat, baby pop, and bring Flyer down to set position. Bases bounce and drive Flyer back up above head into Liberty position.

Flyer

Flyer starts in Liberty position. As Bases squat, Flyer remains tight, and starts to bend knees and put weight to Bases shoulders through Flyer's hands. Flyer taps floor with left foot, pushing off floor to help Bases drive Flyer upward. Flyer will also push through arms, keeping body tight, and locking right leg out as Flyer rides up to Liberty position.

Back Spot

Back Spot starts with hands on Flyer's ankles. On count, Back Spot places Back Spot's left hand on Flyer's seat and squats with Bases, helping to control Flyer for tap. Back Spot will then drive Flyer upward with Bases, using Back Spot's left hand as it thrusts Flyer's seat upward. Back Spot then grabs Flyer's right ankle and assists Flyer to settle in Liberty position.

Double Take Liberty

1. Flyer starts in Liberty

2. Flyer and Base squat for Baby Pop

5. Bases and Flyer squat

6. Bases drive Flyer right back up

Double Take Liberty

3. Flyer starts to bring leg
down as Bases lower

4. Flyer settles into Sponge Position

7. Flyer starts to pull leg back to Liberty,
as Bases continue to drive

8. Flyer hits stunt

Stunt Explanation

Bases

Bases stand facing each other. Flyer will step into Bases' hands. Left Base will grab under Flyer's left foot, under the toe with left hand and Flyer's heel with right hand.

Right Base will grab under Flyer's left foot with left hand under and between Left Base's hands, and Right hand on top of Flyer's Foot, clamping down on Flyer's foot as tight as possible.

On count, the Bases will squat, and drive Flyer upward 6-8 inches above Bases' head and down to Prep level. As the Flyer hits Prep level, the Bases squat and drive the Flyer upward. As the Base drives the Flyer upward, the Bases release the Flyer's left foot and grab Flyer's right foot and lock out at extension. As Bases drive upwards they must also step in as close as possible to one another and lock elbows out.

Flyer

Flyer will place Left foot into Bases' hands and both of Flyer's hands on the shoulder of both Bases. On count, Flyer will squat with Bases and drive through arms to lock out Flyer's left leg. Flyer will then ride above prep level and return to prep level. Bases will squat again and drive Flyer upward, allowing the Flyer to ride up. When Flyer's foot is released, the Flyer will pop up and switch legs. To do this, the Flyer will pull their own weight up through the ribcage, lowering right leg to be caught by Bases and pulling up left leg, being careful not to stomp with right foot.

Note: When doing switch foot tricks, it is strongly recommend to start with weak foot and switch to stronger foot.

Back Spot

Back Spot has left hand on Flyer's left ankle and right hand under Flyer's seat. On count, the Back Spot squats with Bases and Flyer, and drives the seat of the Flyer as fast as possible to help Flyer lock the left leg out. Back Spot will squat with the Bases and again drive upward and release Flyer's Left ankle and grab Flyer's right ankle with both hands. Back Spot will help support and stabilize Flyer while Bases lock their grip in.

Front Spot

Front Spot in this stunt is optional. Front Spots will assist with drive of Flyer to Prep Position, and again to Extension Position.

Pump N Go Switch Foot

Positions

1. Left Base - Black Glove is Left Hand, Front Toe
   - White Glove is Right Hand, Heel

2. Right Base - White Glove is Left Hand under Foot Between Left Base's Hands

3. Right Base - Black Glove is Right Hand, Supports top of Flyer's Foot.

   Lock Foot of Flyer as Tight as Possible

124

Pump N Go Switch Foot

Technique

1. Stunt group Squats

2. Bases drive Flyer upwards, Flyer keeps left leg locked

3. Hit Prep position

4. Bases squat immediately and drive Flyer up

5. In the drive, the Flyer will pull up with the body and switch legs. (Do Not Stomp)

6. Bases release, Catch and Drive

7. Lock out at Heel Stretch

ADVANCED
5

STUNTING

Stunt Explanation

This stunt starts at a Prep Position, ie. Liberty, on page 109.

Bases

Bases start with hands on Flyer's right foot. On count, Bases drive Flyer upward and out of stunt position. Bases rotate ¼ turn counterclockwise, following Flyer into split position. Bases use hands to support Flyer's right foot, upper leg, and lower leg.

Flyer

Flyer starts in Liberty position on Flyer's right leg. On count, Flyer places left leg onto Front Spot's hands into a trigger position. On count, Flyer locks leg and rotates a ¾ turn clockwise and into a right split position with hands on Bases' shoulders (for stability) while keeping weight off the Bases.

Front Spot

Front Spot stands in front of stunt with hands extended. On count, Flyer places left foot onto Front Spot's hands. Front Spot's right hand grabs Flyer's heel with thumb to the back while Front Spot's Left hand grabs Flyer's toe. On count, Front Spot locks arms, rotating Flyer ¾ turn counterclockwise to a split catch. Front Spot's right hand remains on Flyer's heel while Front Spot's left hand supports Flyer's upper leg on descent to split position.

Back Spot

Back Spot starts with hands on Flyer's right leg and ankle, assisting Bases. On count, Back Spot helps drive Flyer upward and out of stunt position. Back Spot rotates ¼ turn counterclockwise, with Bases and follows Flyer into split position. Back Spot reaches for Flyer's right foot and lower leg with Back Spots hands.

Note: This is a transitional stunt.

1. Front Spot grip

2. Flyer places left foot into Front Spots hands

4. Flyer rotates; Front Spot controls rotation

5. Back Spot catches Flyer's right foot

Trigger Split

3. Bases squat and drive Flyer upward

4. Front Spot extends arms as Flyer rotates

7. Flyer reaches for Bases' shoulders. Front Spot and Bases grab for Flyer's thighs

8. Flyer ends in split. Flyer supports weight on Bases' shoulders

Stunt Explanation

Bases

Bases start facing each other with palms up. Flyer stands behind Bases with hands on Bases' shoulders. On count, Bases squat and Flyer places feet on Bases' hands. Bases will drive Flyer upward toward extension. As Flyer nears the top of the drive, the Flyer folds forward into a Pike Position. Bases' release front hand to catch Flyer's back as high as possible to slow Flyer down. When Flyer is at cradle level, the Bases release Flyer's feet with Base's back hands and grab Flyer's back. As Flyer unfolds and steps out of stunt, Bases support Flyer's back, helping Flyer stand upright, until Flyer is standing in front of stunt.

Flyer

Flyer starts with hands on Bases' shoulders. On count, Flyer squats with Bases and Flyer jumps placing feet onto Bases' hands. As Bases drive Flyer upward, Flyer will push off Bases' shoulders and lock out Flyer's legs. As Flyer rides to top of drive, Flyer folds into a pike position and falls into the Bases, rolling onto the Bases' hands. As Bases support Flyer, Flyer opens up, kicking legs out, stepping forward onto the ground (one leg at a time), rolling off the front of the stunt to a standing position in front of stunt.

Back Spot

Back Spot starts with hands on Flyer's waist. On count, Back Spot squats and as Flyer jumps, Back Spot drives Flyer upward releasing Flyer's waist and grabbing Flyer's ankles. When Flyer inverts and rolls, Back Spot remains contacted to the Flyer's ankles. When Flyer lands on Bases and begins to step out of stunt, Back Spot releases Flyer's ankles, one at a time, and helps support Flyer's shoulders until Flyer is upright.

Front Spot

Front Spot stands in front of stunt. As Flyer hits top of ride and bends forward, Front Spot steps to the side and prepares to catch Flyer. Once Front Spot has caught Flyer with both hands, the Front Spot supports Flyer's back and helps Flyer step out and stand upright.

Waterfall

1. Flyer loads into Bases' hands

2. Bases squat

5. At top of Flyer's drive upward, Flyer bends forward

6. Flyer folds into a Pike Position

9. Flyer's one foot is released

10. Flyer steps out of stunt with one leg

130

Waterfall

3. Bases drive Flyer upward

4. Flyer hits extension

7. Flyer grabs own legs; as Bases release front hand to reach for Flyer

8. Bases absorb Flyer

11. Flyer's other foot is released as Bases help Flyer stand up

12. Flyer stands up

Stunt Explanation

Bases

Bases start facing each other, with the Flyer facing the Back Spot. The Flyer puts hands on both Bases' shoulders and Right foot in set position. Right Base's hand grip is as follows: Right hand grabs the Flyer's right toe. The left hand will cross over the right hand and grabs Flyers right heel.

Left Base's hand grip is as follows: Right hand grabs under the Flyer's right foot, and left hand on top of Flyer's right foot. The left hand will only grab the Flyer's foot AFTER the Flyer rotates.

On count, the Bases and Flyer squat and Flyer jumps. As the Bases drive upward, the Flyer will twist counterclockwise and Bases will continue driving above their heads and lock arms out straight in a Heel Stretch Grip. Both Bases will support Flyer's right foot.

Flyer

Flyer starts in front of stunt, facing back wall, with hands on shoulders of Bases. Flyer places right foot in right Base's hands. On count, Flyer squats with Bases, and as Bases drive upward, Flyer pushes off shoulders and begins to turn counterclockwise 180 degrees. It is important the Flyer keeps Right leg locked while riding upward to complete the turn. As Flyer finishes rotation, Flyer pulls Left leg to a heel stretch position.

Back Spot

Back Spot starts facing the Flyer. Back Spot's left hand grabs the ankle of the Flyer, wrapping arm around ankle, and Back Spots Right hand on Flyer's right leg near hamstring. On count Back Spot squats with Bases, and drives Flyer upward, pulling Flyer into stunt locking out Left arm to stabilize Flyer in Heel Stretch. Back Spot will maintain visual and physical contact with the Back Spot throughout the rest of the stunt.

Front Spot

Front Spot starts behind Flyer holding Flyer's rear end and Left ankle. Front Spot drives with Bases, pushing Flyer forward toward the Back Spot, enabling the rotation. When Flyer completes rotation, the Front Spot grabs the Flyer's right ankle helping to stabilizing the stunt.

Half Twist Heel Stretch

Grip Positions

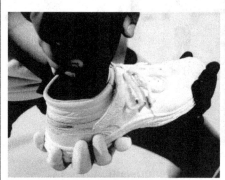

1. Right Base
   Right hand on Flyer's toe - (Black)
   Left hand on Flyer's heel - (White)

2. Left Base
   Left hand under Flyer's heel
   Right hand under Flyer's toe

3. Back Spot
   Left hand on Flyer's ankle
   Right hand on Flyer's hamstring

4. Front Spot
   Right hand on Flyer's seat
   Left hand on Flyer's left ankle.

132

Half Twist Heel Stretch
Technique

1. Flyer places right foot into Bases' hands. Bases and Flyer squat

2. Bases drive Flyer upward

3. Front Spot pushes Flyer toward Back Spot

4. Flyer rotates 180 degrees; Back Spot tightens grip

5. Back Spot locks grip, Front Spot supports Flyer's Right leg

6. Flyer pulls leg upwards, hitting Heel Stretch Position

Stunt Explanation

Bases

Base start facing each other. Right Base grabs Flyer's right foot, with Base's right hand holding Flyer's right toe with Base's fingers pointing toward Base's belly. Base then takes Base's left hand to support Flyer's right heel, and Flyer places hands on Bases' shoulders. On count, Bases and Flyer squat, and Bases will drive Flyer upward, twisting Flyer's foot 360 degrees clockwise and then locking Flyer at extension level.

Secondary Base can be used to drive Flyer's left foot upward. Secondary Base releases left foot and then re-grabs Flyer's left foot when it is in a locked out in an extension position.

Flyer

Flyer starts facing forward and puts Flyer's right foot in Bases' hands. Flyer then places hands on Bases' shoulders. On count, Flyer and Base squat and drive Flyer upward. Flyer stays tight and pushes off Bases' shoulders to twist 360 degrees clockwise, staying under Bases' control. Note: Flyer should not throw body around to twist; Flyer will not stay in the air. Instead, Flyer needs to keep leg locked and in control, and head looking to right.

Back Spot

Back Spot starts behind Flyer and holds Flyer's waist. On count, as Bases and Flyer squat, Back Spot throws Flyer upward from waist and starts Flyer twisting. Back Spot grabs Flyer's ankle at end of rotation. Note: Back Spot may also start by holding Flyer's ankles to launch, but be careful not to hold too tight or it will limit Flyer's twisting.

Front Spot

Front Spot in this stunt is optional. Front Spots will assist with drive of Flyer to Extension Position, helping to support Right Base during the drive upward. Front Spot then provides stability to Flyer.

360 Up

Right Base Grip
Right hand under Flyer's toe with fingertips toward belly.
Left hand under Flyer's heel

Underneath View

3. Bases drive Flyer upwards, Flyer stays tight and begins to rotate

4. Left Base releases Flyer's foot, keeping hands up. Right Base turns Flyer's Right toe 360 degrees around

360 Up

1. Flyer loads foot into Bases' hands

2. Flyer and Bases squat

5. Flyer continues to rotate.

6. Left Base grabs Flyer's left foot

7. Flyer hits Extended Position

Stunt Explanation

Bases

Bases start facing each other. Right Base grabs Flyer's right foot, with Base's right hand holding Flyer's right toe with Base's fingers pointing toward Base's belly. Base then takes Base's left hand to support Flyer's right heel, and Flyer places hand on Bases' shoulders. On count, Bases and Flyer squat, and Bases will drive Flyer upward, twisting Flyer's foot 360 degrees clockwise and then locking Flyer at extension level in a Liberty grip.

Secondary Base can be used to drive Flyer's left foot upward. Secondary Base releases left foot, then re-grabs with right hand under Flyer's right foot and Secondary's Base's left hand on Flyer's shoe laces locking in Flyer's foot tight.

Flyer

Flyer starts facing forward and puts Flyer's right foot in Base's hands. Flyer then places hands on Bases' shoulder. On count, Flyer and Bases squat and drive Flyer upward. Flyer stays tight and pushes off Bases' shoulders to twist 360 degrees clockwise, staying under Bases' control. Note: Flyer should not throw body around to twist; Flyer will not stay in the air. Instead, Flyer needs to keep leg locked and in control.

Back Spot

Back Spot starts behind Flyer and holds Flyer's waist. On count, as Bases and Flyer squat, Back Spot throws Flyer upward from waist and starts Flyer twisting and Back Spot grabs Flyer's ankle at end of rotation. Note: Back Spot may also start by holding Flyer's ankles to launch, but be careful not to hold too tight or it will limit Flyer's twisting.

Back Spot

Front Spot in this stunt is optional. Front Spots will assist with drive of Flyer to Extension Position, helping to support Right Base during the drive upward. Front Spot then provides stability to Flyer.

Right Base Grip
Right hand under Flyer's toe with fingertips toward belly.
Left hand under Flyer's heel

Underneath View

3. Bases drive Flyer upward
   Flyer stays tight and begins to rotate

4. Left Base releases Flyer's foot, keeping hands up.
   Right Base turns Flyer's Right toe 360 degrees around.

136

1. Flyer loads feet into Bases' hands

2. Flyer and Bases squat

4. Flyer continues to rotate

5. **As Flyer finishes rotation, Left Base grabs Flyer's right foot**

7. Flyer hits Liberty Position

Stunt Explanation

This stunt starts in and Extension on page 59.

Bases

Bases start with hands in position 2 and in Extension. Right Base adjusts right hand so that Right Base's hand is under the Flyer's toe with four fingers facing Right Base. On count, Bases drive Flyer up with a baby pop and Right Base starts to rotate Flyer counterclockwise while lowering to a sponge position. The Left Base releases Flyer's foot on the baby pop and helps support the Right Base's hands under the Flyer's foot by helping control the descent of the Flyer.

Flyer

Flyer starts in Extension and on count, the Flyer will ride up with the baby pop and rotate counterclockwise 360 degrees to Sponge Position, grabbing shoulders of Bases on descent to support Flyer's weight. Flyer must stay extremely tight and make sure they do not whip body around on descent, but lower in a controlled manner.

Back Spot

Back Spot starts with hands on Flyer's ankles in extension. Back Spot will move left hand from Flyer's left ankle and place it on the front of Flyer's right ankle. On count, Back Spot will assist Right Base with Flyer's 360 degree descent to sponge position. Back Spot can also assist more novice Flyers by grabbing ankles as soon as Flyer finishes rotation. For more novice Flyer's with Body control issues, Back Spot can catch Flyer's upper leg or seat to help sponge landing of Flyer.

Front Spot

Front Spot in this stunt is optional. Front Spot will assist with baby pop of Flyer through descent into Sponge Position, helping to support Right Base during the lowering. Front Spot then provides stability to Flyer.

360 Down

1. Back Spot holds Flyer's ankles. Front Spot holds Flyer's wrists. Bases hold under Flyer's feet

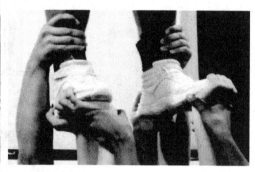

2. Close up of Hand Positions

6. Flyer stays tight as Flyer is rotating

7. Bases control the descent of the Flyer

3. Bases hold Flyer in Extension

4. Bases squat

5. Bases drive Flyer upward Flyer stays tight and begins to rotate

8. Flyer continues rotation

9. Flyer reaches for Bases' shoulders to support own weight

10. Flyer hits end position - Sponge Position

Stunt Explanation

This trick starts in a Heel Stretch but on Flyer's weaker leg on Page 110.

Bases

Bases have Flyer's left ankle in Liberty Position. Bases count 5,6,7, and on count 8, Flyer drops right leg from Heel Stretch position to dead leg position. Then, on count 1, Bases use a small shoulder shrug. Bases then grab Flyer's Right foot and ankle. Bases pop on count 1.

Note: Bases can keep same grip after Flyer switches foot or match grip to Flyer's foot. This is coaches preference.

Flyer

Flyer starts with weaker leg in Heel Stretch position. As Bases count 5,6,7, Flyer drops right leg on count 8 to dead leg Position. Bases will shrug and pop Flyer upward to enable Flyer to pull up Flyer's left leg on count 2 and place straightened right leg for Base's to grab. Flyer then pulls left leg to end position – Heel Stretch

Back Spot

Back Spot supports Flyer's ankle in Heel Stretch position. As Bases shrug and pop Back Spot helps drive Flyer upward and Back Spot then re-grabs Flyer's Right ankle for support and stability of stunt.

Front Spot

Front Spot is optional. Front Spot will assist Bases and help provide stability to Flyer.

Note: Using the counts 5,6,7,8,1,2,3, here is the breakdown to help learn this stunt. 5,6,7 are counts for the group to get aligned. Count 8, Flyer straightens leg to dead leg. On count 1, Bases shrug. On count 2, Bases pop. Count 3, Flyer hits new position.

Tick Tock

1. Flyer starts in Left Heel Stretch

2. Flyer brings Right Leg down

6. After Bases' pop and release Flyer's right foot, they grab Flyer's Left foot

7. Flyer pulls left leg upwards

3. Flyer continues to lower Right Leg

4. Flyer's Right Leg continues to lower

5. As Flyer's Right Leg approaches Left Leg, Flyer shifts weight as Bases Pop

8. Flyer continues swinging Right Leg upward

9. Flyer pulls Left Leg upward, hitting Heel Stretch Position on Right Leg

Stunt Explanation

Bases

Bases start facing each other with Flyer facing forward.

Right Base's left hand grabs Flyer's right hand and Right Base's right hand supports Flyer's right hamstring.

Left Bases' right hand grabs Flyer's left hand and Left Base's left hand supports Flyer's left hamstring.

On count, Flyer will jump up into a Tuck Position. Bases will lock out outside arms and press through legs and drive Flyer upward, through Flyer's legs above Bases' heads. As Flyer rotates, Bases keep arms locked and remain in contact with Flyer until Flyer has been caught by Back Spot and is Stable. Bases now become Spotters.

Flyer

Flyer starts with feet together in front of Back Spot, and hands in grip with Bases. On count, Flyer will jump upward into a tuck position, taking advantage of the Bases by pushing through Flyer's arms for more height while rolling to Hands position. As Flyer completes rotation, Flyer opens up and stands upright on Back Spot's hands. It is important to not over rotate on this stunt.

Back Spot

Back Spot starts with hands on the lower back of Flyer. On count, as Flyer jumps up and into Tuck Position, Back Spot drives Flyer above Bases' heads. As Flyer rotates, Back Spot releases Flyer and catches under Flyer's feet at shoulder level. Back Spot is now Main Base, supporting Flyer.

1. Bases grab Flyer's hands with inside hand and Flyer's Hamstrings with other hand

2. Left Base hand grip with Flyer. Left Base's right hand grips with Flyer's left hand

   Right is same grip on opposite side

6. Flyer jumps upward into a Tuck

7. Bases drive Flyer's Legs above Back Spot's head

3. Bases set arm positions

4. Bases set arm positions
Front View

5. Bases and Flyer squat

8. Back Spot grabs Flyer's feet and
becomes Main Base
Bases hold Flyer's hands until Flyer
is stable to stand upright

9. Flyer stands up, hitting stunt
Bases keep hands up for safety

DISMOUNTS
6
STUNTING

Stunt Explanation

Bases

Bases start by holding Flyers feet at shoulder height. Bases bring Flyer's feet together. The Bases then release Flyer's feet and grab Flyer's waist and help Flyer to the ground.

Flyer

Flyer starts in High V and clasps hands together over head as Bases bring feet together. As feet are released, Flyer prepares to land on the ground with bended knees. Flyer then stands up.

Back Spot

Back Spot starts by holding Flyer's ankles as feet are brought together. Back Spot releases Flyer's ankles and grabs waist as Flyer is released to the ground. On way down, Back Spot slows Flyer down by grabbing Flyer's waist.

The Purpose of the Pencil Drop is to return the flyer safely to the ground from various stunts. It is a more controlled landing.

Pencil Drop

1. Hit High V

2. Arms together, feet together

3. Release feet

4. Grab waist

Pencil Drop

Cradle Catches

1. Traditional

This is the more common cradle.
The Bases support the Flyer's Back and Legs
The Back Spot supports under the Flyer's armpits
The Flyer supports their own weight on Bases' shoulders
The Front Spot is not needed, but if used, supports Flyer's lower legs (appearance only)

2. Hollow Body

THIS IS ONLY FOR ADVANCED BASES!
This technique is mainly used for double down skills to protect the Bases
The Flyer pikes mildly into a hollow or rod position
Flyer's arms and legs are together in a hollow body position
Bases support Flyer's Back and Legs - Flyer DOES NOT support her own weight
Back Spot supports Flyers' back

Stunt Explanation

Bases

Bases start holding feet of Flyer, as in most stunts. On count, Bases will squat and then pop the Flyer using the strength in their legs. As the Bases pop, their arms should drive the Flyer straight up. As the Bases drive Flyer, the Bases should step in for the catch. Bases keep hands, palms up, to prepare to catch Flyer as Flyer descends. Bases should catch the Flyer at the highest point possible, with their arms cradling Flyer's back and legs.

Flyer

Flyer starts with feet in Bases' hands. As the Bases squat and drive, the Flyer should pull upward with arms in Touchdown Position, staying tight. After the Flyer's feet are released, the Flyer slightly arches her back with her stomach pulling toward the ceiling until the Flyer hits the very top of the cradle, (the point where she feels herself coming down). The Flyer should pull her body to a V position, not a pike position. To do this, the Flyer bends at hips, keeping legs straight and toes pointed. When the Flyer makes contact with the Bases, the Flyer puts one arm around each Base to assist in the catch.and support own weight.

Back Spot

Back Spot starts with hands on Flyer's ankles. Back Spot will squat with Bases and pop Flyer upward, releasing the ankles of the Flyer when Back Spot's arms are locked out, leaving arms in the air until the Flyer descends. As the Flyer descends, the Back Spot ensures the safety of the Flyer by keeping the Back Spots arms straight forward and toward the front of stunt. As the Flyer makes contact, the Back Spot scoops under the Flyer's armpits. In addition, as the Flyer descends, it is important that the Back Spot keeps her head back to prevent knocking heads with the Flyer, but still keeping visual contact with the Flyer.

Basic Cradle

1. Hit High V

2. Bases squat and pop Flyer on count

3. Flyer rides up, pulling shoulders up for more height

4. Bases catch Flyer high

5. Back Spot grabs under Flyer's armpits

6. Bases catch Flyer in Cradle Position

Stunt Explanation

Bases

Bases start holding feet of Flyer, as in most stunts. On count, Bases will squat and then pop the Flyer using the strength in their legs. As the Bases pop, their arms should drive the Flyer straight up. As the Bases drive Flyer, the Bases should step in for the catch. Bases keep their hands, palms up, to prepare to catch Flyer as Flyer descends. Bases should catch the Flyer at the highest point possible, with their arms cradling Flyer's back and legs.

Flyer

Flyer starts with feet in Bases' hands. As the Bases squat and drive, the Flyer should pull shoulders upward, slapping arms to side of Flyer's body, staying tight. After the Flyer's feet are released, the Flyer slightly arches her back with her stomach pulling toward the ceiling until the Flyer hits the very top of the cradle, (the point where she feels herself coming down). The Flyer should mildly arch, pulling body to a V position, not a pike position. To do this, the Flyer bends at hips, keeping legs straight and toes pointed. When the Flyer makes contact with the Bases, the Flyer puts one arm around each Base to assist in the catch.

Back Spot

Back Spot starts with hands on Flyer's ankles. Back Spot will squat with Bases and pop Flyer upward releasing the ankles of the Flyer when Back Spot's arms are locked out, leaving arms in the air until the Flyer descends. As the Flyer descends, the Back Spot ensures the safety, of the Flyer by keeping the Back Spot's arms straight forward and toward the front of stunt. As the Flyer makes contact, the Back Spot scoops under the Flyer's armpits to, absorbing the catch. Back Spot should keep hands in Blades, thumbs in, to protect Flyer and Back Spot on Catch. In addition, as the Flyer descends, it is important that the Back Spot keeps her head back to prevent knocking heads with the Flyer, but still keeping visual contact with the Flyer.

Competition Cradle

1. Bases squat

2. Bases drive Flyer through extension. Bases' hands remain up after release of Flyer Flyer pulls hands to hips with body tight and in a mild arch

5. Flyer catches Bases' shoulders Back Spot reaches high and absorbs Flyer, catching under armpits

Competition Cradle

3. Bases and Back Spot release
   Flyer's feet

4. Flyer starts to break arch for cradle

6. Side View
   Cradle

7. Front View
   Cradle

Stunt Explanation

This stunt starts in a prep position page 54.

Bases

Bases start with hands on Flyer's feet. On count, Bases squat and drive Flyer upward through extension. Flyer is released at top of drive and Bases' hands remain up awaiting Flyer. As Flyer comes down, Bases grab Flyer's back and legs, keeping Bases' head straight and back to prevent hitting heads with opposite Base.

Flyer

Flyer starts in prep position. On count, as Bases' are driving Flyer upward, Flyer rides up and Flyer will drop left arm to left hip and pull right arm to left hip to rotate counterclockwise in a prone position. As roll finishes 360 degrees, Flyer sits up into a "V" cradle position, hollowing body out and lands in cradle, wrapping arms around Bases' shoulders.

Back Spot

Back Spot stands behind Flyer, holding Flyer's ankles. On count, Back Spot squats and throws Flyer upward, extending Back Spot's arms and leaving them high above Back Spot's head with palms upward. As Flyer returns, Back Spot grabs under Flyer's armpits and keeps Back Spot's head back to prevent hitting heads with Flyer. Back Spot must ensure the safety of Flyer's head, neck, and back while catching Flyer. Back Spot should also maintain visual contact with Flyer in case Flyer's position in the air changes.

Front Spot

Front Spot stands in front of Flyer holding Bases' wrists. Front Spot helps with drive and with catching of Flyer. This Spot is optional.

Full Down

1. Hit High V

2. Bases squat and prepare to drive

6. Flyer continues rotation, staying tight

7. As rotation nears 360 degrees, Flyer prepares to sit up

3. As Bases drive Flyer upward, Flyer drops left arm to Flyer's left hip

4. As Bases release, Flyer pulls with right arm to Flyer's left hip

5. Flyer continues counterclockwise rotation.

8. Bases absorbs cradle
Front View

9. Bases absorb cradle
Side View

Stunt Explanation

Bases

This stunt starts in a prep position page 54.

Bases

Bases start with hands on Flyer's feet. On count, Bases squat and drive Flyer upward through extension. Flyer is released at top of drive and Bases' hands remain up awaiting Flyer. As Flyer comes down, Bases grab Flyer's back and legs, keeping Bases' head straight and back to prevent hitting heads with opposite Base.

Flyer

On count, as Bases are driving Flyer upward, Flyer rides up and Flyer will drop left arm to left hip and pull right arm to left hip to rotate counter-clockwise in a twisting position. As roll finishes 2 full rotations, Flyer sits up into a "V" cradle position, hollowing body out and landing in cradle, wrapping arms around Bases' shoulders. Note: For great double downs, Flyer should be 1 ½ rotations around before descending into cradle.

Back Spot

Back Spot stands behind Flyer, holding Flyer's ankles. On count, Back Spot squats and throws Flyer upward, extending Back Spot's arms and leaving them high above Back Spot's head with palms upward. As Flyer returns, Back Spot grabs under Flyer's armpits and keeps Back Spot's head back to prevent hitting heads with Flyer. Back Spot must ensure the safety of Flyer's head, neck, and back while catching Flyer. Back Spot should also maintain visual contact with Flyer in case Flyer's position in the air changes.

Front Spot

Front Spot stands in front of Flyer holding Bases' wrists. Front Spot helps with drive and with catching of Flyer. Front Spot is optional.

Double Down

1. Hit High V

2. Bases squat and prepare to drive

6. Flyer continues rotation, staying tight

7. As rotation nears 2 full rotations, Flyer prepares to sit up

154

Double Down

3. As Bases drive Flyer upward, Flyer drops left arm to Flyer's left hip

4. As Bases release, Flyer pulls with right arms to Flyer's left hip

5. Flyer continues counterclockwise rotation

8. Bases step in extra close for safety

9. Bases absorb cradle

Stunt Explanation

Flyer can use either a 1 foot load or 2 foot jump in.

Bases

Bases Hand grip is: Left Base has Right hand on Left wrist and Left hand on Right Base's Right hand. Right Base has Right hand on Left wrist and Left hand on Left Base's Right wrist. Flyer has hands on Bases' shoulders with elbows up. On count, Flyer jumps and puts both feet together onto Bases' hands. Bases keep grip and arms loose. On count, Bases squat and thrust Flyer with arms, snapping arms to ceiling as quick as possible (Speed is the trick). Bases will leave arms extended and palms up to catch Flyer. As Flyer comes down, Bases grab Flyer's back and legs, keeping Bases' head straight and back to prevent hitting heads with opposite Base.

Flyer

Flyer starts with hands on Bases' shoulders and elbows up. Back Spot has hands on Flyer's waist. On count, Flyer squats, jumps up, and places both feet together onto Bases' hands. As Bases squat and drive Flyer upward, Flyer pushes through hands on Bases' shoulders and pushes through Flyer's legs. Flyer should lock legs as Flyer rides to top. As Flyer hits top, Flyer mildly arches and rides down in a "V" cradle position, hollowing body out and lands in cradle, wrapping arms around Bases' shoulders.

Back Spot

Back Spot stands behind Flyer, holding Flyer's waist. On count, Back Spot squats with Flyer and controls Flyer onto Bases' hands. As Flyer loads, Back Spot places hands under Bases' grip, pushing up on Base's hands for more power. Back Spot then squats with Bases and throws Flyer upward, extending Back Spot's arms and leaving them high above Back Spot's head with palms upwards. As Flyer returns, Back Spot grabs under Flyer's armpits and keeps Back Spot's head back to prevent hitting heads with Flyer. Back Spot must ensure the safety of Flyer's head, neck, and back while catching Flyer. Back Spot should also maintain visual contact with Flyer in case Flyer's position in the air changes.

Straight Basket

1. Bases set grip

2. Flyer places hands on Bases' shoulders.
Flyer places one foot on Bases' hands,
Front View

6. Bases snap arms and Flyer rides to top (Shown with optional Front Spot)

7. Bases keep arms up

156

3. Flyer jumps and brings
   feet together on Bases'
   hands.
   DO NOT STOMP!
Side View-optional Front Spot

4. Bases squat
   Back Spot moves hands
   under Bases' hands

5. Start to drive through legs,
   begin thrusting Flyer upwards

8. Flyer hits "v" position
   If using Front Spot:
   Front Spot moves to one
   side to assist with catching
   Flyer's feet

9. Bases step in for cradle

10. Bases catch in cradle
    and Back Spot absorbs Flyer

Stunt Explanation

Flyer can use either a 1 foot load or 2 foot jump in.

Bases

Bases Hand grip is: Left Base has Right hand on Left wrist and Left hand on Right Base's Right hand. Right Base has Right hand on Left wrist and Left hand on Left Base's Right wrist. Flyer has hands on Bases' shoulders with elbows up. On count, Flyer jumps and puts both feet together onto Bases' hands. Bases keep grip and arms loose. On count, Bases squat and thrust Flyer with arms, snapping arms to ceiling as quick as possible (Speed is the trick). Bases will leave arms extended and palms up to catch Flyer. As Flyer comes down, Bases grab Flyer's back and legs, keeping Bases' head straight and back to prevent hitting heads with opposite Base.

Flyer

Flyer starts with hands on Bases' shoulders and elbows up. Back Spot has hands on Flyer's waist. On count, Flyer squats, jumps up, and places both feet together onto Bases' hands. As Bases squat and drive Flyer upward, Flyer pushes through hands on Base's shoulders and pushes through Flyer's legs. At top, Flyer pulls legs up and snaps into Toe Touch Position and then snaps back into a mild arch and rides down in a "V" cradle position, hollowing body out and lands in cradle, wrapping arms around Bases' shoulders.

Back Spot

Back Spot stands behind Flyer, holding Flyer's waist. On count, Back Spot squats with Flyer and controls Flyer onto Bases' hands. As Flyer loads, Back Spot places hands under Bases' grip, pushing up on Bases' hands for more power. Back Spot then squats with Bases and throws Flyer upward, extending Back Spot's arms and leaving them high above Back Spot's head with palms upwards. As Flyer returns, Back Spot grabs under Flyer's armpits and keeps Back Spot's head back to prevent hitting heads with Flyer. Back Spot must ensure the safety of Flyer's head, neck, and back while catching Flyer. Back Spot should also maintain visual contact with Flyer in case Flyer's position in the air changes.

Toe Touch Basket

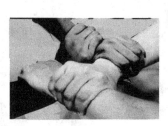

1. Bases set grip

2. Stunt group squats

6. Flyer arches out

Side View & with optional Front Spot

7. Flyer does crunch, changing body position to a "V"

3. Back Spot grabs underneath Bases' hands. Flyer has both feet on Bases' hands

4. Flyer rides upward

5. Flyer pulls legs upward hitting Toe Touch Position

8. Bases and Back Spot catch Flyer in cradle

9. Bases and Back Spot cradle with optional Front Spot

Stunt Explanation

Bases

Flyer can use either a 1 foot load or 2 foot jump in. See Pg 156 for hand grip;

Bases Hand grip is: Left Base has Right hand on Left wrist and Left hand on Right Base's Right hand. Right Base has Right hand on Left wrist and Left hand on Left Base's Right wrist. Flyer has hands on Bases' shoulders with elbows up. On count, Flyer jumps and puts both feet together onto Bases' hands. Bases keep grip and arms loose. On count, Bases squat and thrust Flyer with arms, snapping arms to ceiling as quick as possible (Speed is the trick). Bases will leave arms extended and palms up to catch Flyer. As Flyer comes down, Bases grab Flyer's back and legs, keeping Bases' head straight and back to prevent hitting heads with opposite Base.

Flyer

Flyer starts with hands on Bases' shoulders and elbows up. Back Spot has hands on Flyer's waist. On count, Flyer squats, jumps up, and places both feet together onto Bases' hands. As Bases squat and drive Flyer upward, Flyer pushes through hands on Bases' shoulders and pushes through Flyer's legs. At top, Flyer pulls legs up and folds into Pike Position and snaps into a mild arch and rides down in a "V" cradle position, hollowing body out and lands in cradle, wrapping arms around Bases' shoulders.

Back Spot

Back Spot stands behind Flyer, holding Flyer's waist. On count, Back Spot squats with Flyer and controls Flyer onto Bases' hands. As Flyer loads, Back Spot places hands under Bases' grip, pushing up on Bases' hands for more power. Back Spot then squats with Bases and throws Flyer upward, extending Back Spot's arms and leaving them high above Back Spot's head with palms upwards. As Flyer returns, Back Spot grabs under Flyer's armpits and keeps Back Spot's head back to prevent hitting heads with Flyer. Back Spot must ensure the safety of Flyer's head, neck, and back while catching Flyer. Back Spot should also maintain visual contact with Flyer in case Flyer's position in the air changes.

Pike Basket

1. Stunt group squats

2. Back Spot grabs underneath Bases' hands. Flyer has both feet on Bases' hands

3. Flyer rides upward and hits Pike Position

4. Flyer arches out

5. Flyer does crunch, changing body position to a "V"

6. Bases and Back Spot cradle Flyer

Stunt Explanation

Bases

Flyer can use either a 1 foot load or 2 foot jump in. See Pg 156 for hand grip; Bases Hand grip is: Left Base has Right hand on Left wrist and Left hand on Right Base's Right hand. Right Base has Right hand on Left wrist and Left hand on Left Base's Right wrist. Flyer has hands on Bases' shoulders with elbows up. On count, Flyer jumps and puts both feet together onto Bases' hands. Bases keep grip and arms loose. On count, Bases squat and thrust Flyer with arms, snapping arms to ceiling as quick as possible (Speed is the trick). Bases will leave arms extended and palms up to catch Flyer. As Flyer comes down, Bases grab Flyer's back and legs, keeping Bases' head straight and back to prevent hitting heads with opposite Base.

Flyer

Flyer starts with hands on Bases' shoulders and elbows up. Back Spot has hands on Flyer's waist. On count, Flyer squats, jumps up, and places both feet together onto Bases' hands. As Bases squat and drive Flyer upward, Flyer pushes through hands on Bases' shoulders and pushes through Flyer's legs. Flyer rides to top, pulling 1 leg upward, then snaps legs together out to a mild arch and ends in a "V" cradle position, hollowing body out and land in a cradle, wrapping arms around Bases' shoulders.

Back Spot

Back Spot stands behind Flyer, holding Flyer's waist. On count, Back Spot squats with Flyer and controls Flyer onto Bases' hands. As Flyer loads, Back Spot places hands under Bases' grip, pushing up on Bases' hands for more power. Back Spot then squats with Bases and throws Flyer upward, extending Back Spot's arms and leaving them high above Back Spot's head with palms upwards. As Flyer returns, Back Spot grabs under Flyer's armpits and keeps Back Spot's head back to prevent hitting heads with Flyer. Back Spot must ensure the safety of Flyer's head, neck, and back while catching Flyer. Back Spot should also maintain visual contact with Flyer in case Flyer's position in the air changes.

Kick Basket

1. Stunt group squats

2. Back Spot grabs underneath Bases' hands, Flyer has both feet on Bases' hands

3. Flyer rides upward in Kick Position

4. Flyer arches out

5. Flyer does crunch, changing body position to a "V"

6. Bases and Back Spot cradle Flyer

161

Stunt Explanation

Bases

Flyer can use either a 1 foot load or 2 foot jump in. See Pg 156 for hand grip. Bases Hand grip is: Left Base has Right hand on Left wrist and Left hand on Right Base's Right hand. Right Base has Right hand on Left wrist and Left hand on Left Base's Right wrist. Flyer has hands on Bases' shoulders with elbows up. On count, Flyer jumps and puts both feet together onto Bases' hands. Bases keep grip and arms loose. On count, Bases squat and thrust Flyer with arms, snapping arms to ceiling as quick as possible (Speed is the trick). Bases will leave arms extended and palms up to catch Flyer. As Flyer comes down, Bases grab Flyer's back and legs, keeping Bases' head straight and back to prevent hitting heads with opposite Base.

Flyer

Flyer starts with hands on Bases' shoulders and elbows up. Back Spot has hands on Flyer's waist. On count, Flyer squats, jumps up, and places both feet together onto Bases' hands. As Bases squat and drive Flyer upward, Flyer pushes through hands on Bases' shoulders and pushes through Flyer's legs. Flyer rides to top, pulling knees to a tuck position, then snaps out to mild arch and ends in a "V" cradle position, hollowing body out and land in cradle, wrapping arms around Bases' shoulders.

Back Spot

Back Spot stands behind Flyer, holding Flyer's waist. On count, Back Spot squats with Flyer and controls Flyer onto Bases' hands. As Flyer loads, Back Spot places hands under Bases' grip, pushing up on Bases' hands for more power. Back Spot then squats with Bases and throws Flyer upward, extending Back Spot's arms and leaving them high above Back Spot's head with palms upwards. As Flyer returns, Back Spot grabs under Flyer's armpits and keeps Back Spot's head back to prevent hitting heads with Flyer. Back Spot must ensure the safety of Flyer's head, neck, and back while catching Flyer. Back Spot should also maintain visual contact with Flyer in case Flyer's position in the air changes.

Ball Basket

1. Stunt group squats

2. Back Spot grabs underneath Bases' hands. Flyer has both feet on Bases' hands

3. Flyer rides upward in Ball Position

4. Flyer arches out

5. Flyer does crunch, changing body position to a "V"

6. Bases and Back Spot cradle Flyer

Stunt Explanation

Bases

Flyer can use either a 1 foot load or 2 foot jump in. See Pg 156 for hand grip. Bases Hand grip is: Left Base has Right hand on Left wrist and Left hand on Right Base's Right hand. Right Base has Right hand on Left wrist and Left hand on Left Base's Right wrist. Flyer has hands on Bases' shoulders with elbows up. On count, Flyer jumps and puts both feet together onto Bases' hands. Bases keep grip and arms loose. On count, Bases squat and thrust Flyer with arms, snapping arms to ceiling as quick as possible (Speed is the trick). Bases will leave arms extended and palms up to catch Flyer. As Flyer comes down, Bases grab Flyer's back and legs, keeping Bases' head straight and back to prevent hitting heads with opposite Base.

Flyer

Flyer starts with hands on Bases' shoulders and elbows up. Back Spot has hands on Flyer's waist. On count, Flyer squats, jumps up, and places both feet together onto Bases' hands. As Bases squat and drive Flyer upward, Flyer pushes through hands on Bases' shoulders and pushes through Flyer's legs. Flyer rides to top, pulling knees to chest and then snaps out to 'X' position with mild arch. Flyer then closes legs, starts to hollow body out, and lands in cradle, wrapping arms around Bases' shoulders.

Back Spot

Back Spot stands behind Flyer, holding Flyer's waist. On count, Back Spot squats with Flyer and controls Flyer onto Bases' hands. As Flyer loads, Back Spot places hands under Bases' grip, pushing up on Bases' hands for more power. Back Spot then squats with Bases and throws Flyer upward, extending Back Spot's arms and leaving them high above Back Spot's head with palms upwards. As Flyer returns, Back Spot grabs under Flyer's armpits and keeps Back Spot's head back to prevent hitting heads with Flyer. Back Spot must ensure the safety of Flyer's head, neck, and back while catching Flyer. Back Spot should also maintain visual contact with Flyer in case Flyer's position in the air changes.

Ball X Basket

1. Stunt group squats

2. Back Spot grabs underneath Bases' hands. Flyer has both feet on Bases' hands

3. Flyer rides upward in Ball Position

4. Flyer arches out in an "X" position; Arms in High V Legs are straddled

5. Flyer does crunch, changing body position to a "V"

6. Bases and Back Spot cradle Flyer

163

Stunt Explanation

Bases

Flyer can use either a 1 foot load or 2 foot jump in. See pg 156 for hand grip.

Bases start facing right wall. Bases Hand grip is: Left Base has Right hand on Left wrist and Left hand on Right Base's Right hand. Right Base has Right hand on Left wrist and Left hand on Left Base's Right wrist. Flyer has hands on Bases' shoulders with elbows up. On count, Flyer jumps and puts both feet together onto Base's hands. Bases keep grip and arms loose. On count, Bases squat and thrust Flyer with arms, snapping arms to ceiling as quick as possible (Speed is the trick). After throw, Bases' group will rotate ¼ to front. Bases will leave arms extended and palms up to catch Flyer. As Flyer comes down, Bases grab Flyer's back and legs, keeping Bases' head straight and back to prevent hitting heads with opposite Base.

Flyer

Flyer starts with hands on Bases' shoulders and elbows up, facing right wall. Back Spot has hands on Flyer's waist. On count, Flyer squats, jumps up, and places both feet together onto Bases' hands. As Bases squat and drive Flyer upward, Flyer pushes through hands on Bases' shoulders and pushes through Flyer's legs. During ride, Flyer will turn ¼ to front, hitting a Heel Stretch kick Position. Flyer then pulls left arm down and right arm and leg over to a Full Down (360 degree roll). After rotation, Flyer will end in a "V" cradle position, hollowing body out and lands in cradle, wrapping arms around Bases' shoulders.

Back Spot

Back Spot stands behind Flyer, holding Flyer's waist. On count, Back Spot squats with Flyer and controls Flyer onto Bases' hands. As Flyer loads, Back Spot places hands under Bases' grip, pushing up on Bases' hands for more power. Back Spot then squats with Bases and throws Flyer upward, extending Back Spot's arms and leaving them high above Back Spot's head with palms upward, following Bases and turning a ¼ turn counterclockwise to face the crowd. As Flyer returns, Back Spot grabs under Flyer's armpits and keeps Back Spot's head back to prevent hitting heads with Flyer. Back Spot must ensure the safety of Flyer's head, neck, and back while catching Flyer. Back Spot should also maintain visual contact with Flyer in case Flyer's position in the air changes.

Kick Full Basket

1. Flyer loads, Bases set grip

2. Bases squat

6. Flyer closes legs, starts to turn

7. Flyer starts Full Down

164

Kick Full Basket

3. Bases drive Flyer upward

4. Flyer rides up, faces forward and kicks as high as possible

5. Flyer hits Kick Position

8. Flyer begins to open for cradle

9. Bases absorb Flyer in cradle

10. Cradle

CO-ED STUNTS

STUNTING 7

Co-ed Positions

Hands

Extension

Grin and Bear It

Cupie/Awesome

Reverse Hands
(Rear View)

Reverse Hands
(Front View)

Liberty Arabesque

High Torch Arabesque

Heel Stretch

Bow and Arrow

Co-ed Positions

Liberty
(Front View)

Liberty
(Side View)

Scorpion

Dead Leg

Grab foot with hand behind back

Pull leg up overhead

Scale

Dead Leg

Grab Leg with hand behind back

Extend Leg behind

Stunt Explanation

This occurs at the end of the stunt to exit a stunt. It can be done from 1 or 2 legged co-ed stunts at half or extension.

Base

Base starts with hand(s) on Flyer's feet, on count drive Flyer upward through an extension, releasing Flyer. Base will turn Flyer a ¼ turn to the right, following Flyer at all times. Base keeps arms up as high as possible while waiting for Flyer, keeping visual contact with the Flyer the entire time. As the Flyer lands in Base's arms, Base grabs Flyer's back and legs absorbing the landing, and pulling Flyer into Base.

Flyer

Flyer starts with 1 or 2 feet on Base's hands. On count Flyer will ride upward as Base pops Flyer. Flyer pulls up, hips up to ride the pop. As the Flyer starts to descend, the Flyer sits up in a "V" cradle position. As Base catches Flyer, Flyer places BOTH arms around Base's shoulders and neck to help take weight off the Base and to help support Flyer.

Back Spot

Back Spot stands at back right corner of Base and is there to assist if any problems occur. Back Spot visually follows Flyer, ensuring the safety of the head, back, and neck of Flyer.

Co-ed Cradles

1. Start in Hands Position

2. Flyer and Base squat

3. After Drive, Flyer starts to sit on way down. Base keeps arms extended reaching for Flyer

4. Base catches Flyer nice and high

5. Base absorbs cradle

Co-ed Cradles

Stunt Explanation

Base

Base stands with left leg forward in lunge position, facing Flyer. As Flyer puts Left foot into Base's hip pocket, Base grabs Flyer's left ankle with Base's Left hand. The Base's right hand goes under the Flyer's seat. On count, Base and Flyer squat, Base drives Flyer upward using legs and arms. As Base drives Flyer upward, the Flyer sits on the Base's right hand and the Base drives the Flyer's left ankle upward. The Base locks out the right arm, after Flyer turns clockwise to face the front, keeping Base's arm close to the Base's head. The Base also pulls up on Flyer's left ankle to take weight off Base's right arm.

Flyer

Flyer puts left foot into hip pocket of Base's left leg, facing Base. Flyer's hands go on shoulders of the Base. On count, Flyer will squat with Base and push off the ground with Flyer's left leg and push through Base's shoulders to drive Flyer upward. As Base drives up, the Flyer should look down the back of Base and turn clockwise halfway to a seated position with Flyer's left leg locked and Flyer's Right leg in Liberty position. Be careful not to push bent leg into Base's arm.

Back Spot

Back Spot stands at back right corner of Base and is there to assist if any problems occur. Back Spot can help lock Base's arm out if needed.

Dismount

Flyer can be popped off front and brought down with Base's hands on Flyer's waist or through a cradle.

Walk Chair

Positions

1. Flyer puts Left foot in Base's hip pocket, Flyer's arms on Base's shoulders

2. Base uses left hand to grab Base's right ankle

3. Base uses right hand to hold Flyer's seat

172

1. Base and Flyer squat, prepare to drive

2. Base drives Flyer upward. Flyer sits on Base's hand and Back Spot can assist for stability

3. On count, Base pops Flyer off toward front

4. Base assists Flyer down, controlling landing

Stunt Explanation

Base
Base stands behind Flyer and grabs Flyer by hip bones or waist. On count, Base and Flyer will squat, driving through legs, and driving Flyer upward above Base's head, snapping through the wrists at top. Base's Right hand will support Flyer's seat. Base's Left hand will grab Flyer's Left ankle, and brings it to the center of Base's Chest.

Flyer
Flyer stands with feet together in front of Base with Flyer's hands on Base's wrists. On count, Flyer and Base squat and Flyer will put all weight on Base's wrists. As Base drives Flyer upward, Flyer will ride to top and snap off Base's wrists. Flyer will sit on Base's hand and as Flyer lands, Flyer bends Right leg and lock Flyer's left leg in a Liberty position.

Back Spot
Back Spot stands at back right corner of Base and is there to assist if any problems occur. Back Spot can help lock Base's arm out if needed.

Dismount
Flyer can be popped off front and brought down with Base's hands on Flyer's waist and Flyer's hands on Base's wrists or through a cradle.

1. Base grabs Flyer's waist. Flyer grab's Base's wrists

2. Base and Flyer squat

3. Base tosses Flyer upward Flyer snaps off Base's wrists

4. Base grabs Flyer's seat and hits chair

5. Base pops Flyer toward front. Flyer reaches for Base's wrists

6. Base supports Flyer down for landing

Stunt Explanation

This stunt starts from chair position as on page 174.

Base

Base has Flyer in Chair Position with Left hand on Flyer's left ankle and right hand on Flyer's seat. The Base will shift Base's left hand to the middle of Flyer's left foot. On count, Base will squat and drive Flyer upward, through Flyer's locked leg, using Base's legs to snap through shoulder above Base's head. As Flyer rides upward, Base takes Base's right hand and grabs under Flyer's right foot, driving Flyer above Base's head and settling in hands position.

Flyer

Flyer starts with seat on Base's hand and Flyer's Left foot on Base's left hand. On count, the Base squats and drives Flyer upward. The Flyer must keep Flyer's left leg locked, to allow Base to drive Flyer upward. As Flyer rides upward, Flyer must straighten Flyer's right leg so that Base can grab Flyer's right foot and settle in hands position.

Back Spot

Back Spot stands at back right corner of Base and is there to assist if any problems occur. Back Spot visually follows Flyer ensuring the safety of the head, back, and neck of Flyer. If Back Spot is needed, Back Spot will hold Flyer's Left ankle to take pressure off Base as Flyer is driven upward.

1. Base grabs Flyer's waist, Flyer grabs Base's wrists

2. Flyer and Base squat

5. Base releases Flyer's ankle and grabs under Flyer's left foot.

6. Base squats

3. Base drives Flyer upward

4. Flyer hits Chair position

7. Base drives Flyer above
   Base's head; Flyer stands up

8. Flyer hits stunt

Stunt Explanation

Base

Base starts standing shoulder to shoulder with Flyer, with Flyer on Base's Right. Base will grab Flyer's right inner thigh with Base's right hand. Base's left hand grabs the inside of Flyer's rib cage (left side), Base's thumb should be down with fingers to the back. Flyer will place Flyer's left hand on Base's left shoulder. On count, Flyer will jump and Base will squat, lifting Flyer above Base's head in power press position, locking out both of Base's arms.

Flyer

Flyer stands shoulder to shoulder with Base on Flyer's Left side. Base will grab Flyer's inner thigh and rib cage, and Flyer places left hand on Base's left shoulder. On count, Flyer jumps, putting weight on Base's shoulder with Flyer's left hand. As Base is driving up it is important for Flyer to squeeze inner thighs together and stay tight, hips up and locked in position. Flyer's Right arm is straight up in the air.

Back Spot

Back Spot stands at back left corner of Base and is there to assist if any problems occur. Back Spot can help lock Bases arm out if needed. Back Spots responsibility in this stunt is to protect head, neck, and back, as in all stunts, but especially in this stunt.

Dismount

The dismount of this stunt is a roll down. On count, the Flyer will take Flyer's right arm which is in a T position and punch through toward Base's left bicep. As this happens, the Base curls left arm to bicep curl, in which the Flyer's right arm will hook into. The Base's right arm will just roll through and maintain hold on Flyer's inner thigh. The Back Spot will be on left side toward front of Base, following roll through ensuring the hook is successful spotting the head, back and neck.

Sailor

Positions

1. Base grabs Flyer's inner thigh of right leg with Base's Right hand, thumb forward.
   Flyer grabs Base's left shoulder with Flyer's left hand

2. Base grabs Flyer's left side, around rib cage, with Base's left hand, thumb forward

Technique

1. Set grip

2. Base and Flyer squat

3. Base presses Flyer up.
   Flyer keeps body tight and straight

4. Base holds Flyer overhead

5. Flyer punches down and begins to turn

6. Base catches Flyer -
   Base's right hand remains on Flyer's inner thigh.
   Base's left arm hooks Flyer's right arm

Stunt Explanation

Base

Base starts with Flyer in front of Base. Base squats down and grabs Flyer's left ankle with Base's left hand. Base will then place right hand on the small of Flyer's back. On count, the Flyer will jump upward. Base will pull hard with the left arm and support the Flyer above Base's head with Base's right arm, keeping Base's left arm straight and in front to keep tension on the stunt.

Flyer

Flyer starts with left leg slightly bent, standing on Flyer's right leg and in front of Base. On count, Flyer will jump up and lean back to create an arch in Flyer's back so Base can get a better grip. Flyer's Left leg straightens and Flyer's right leg will bend and end in a liberty position. Flyer's arms end stunt in a T position, but other positions are also acceptable.

Back Spot

Back Spot will spot back right or left corner of stunt- side is optional and coaches preference. Back Spot will make sure Flyer rides up in a controlled manner. Once Flyer is in back arch, Back Spot goes to right back corner of stunt to assist with cradle and help spot head, neck, and back appropriately.

Base will squat and drive through Base's legs, thrusting Flyer up and away, keeping arms up and catching Flyer in a basic cradle position. Flyer remains tight as Base pops Flyer and Flyer slightly arches her back with her stomach, pulling toward the ceiling until the Flyer hits the very top of the cradle, (the point where she feels herself coming down). The Flyer should pull her body to a V position, not a pike position. To do this, the Flyer bends at her hips, keeping legs straight and toes pointed. When the Flyer makes contact with the Base, the Flyer puts both arms around Base to assist in the catch.

Back Arch

1. Base grabs Flyer's left ankle with Base's left hand
   Base grabs Flyer's "small of the back'" with Base's right hand

4. Base drives Flyer upward; Flyer pulls up right knee

5. Flyer remains tight as Base gets under stunt; Base pushing up on Flyer's back

8. Base gets both arms up to catch Flyer, Flyer remains tight.

Back Arch

2. Base squats and sets grip

3. Flyer squats

6. Base supports Flyer as
   Flyer hits position

7. Dismount - Flyer straightens
   right leg

9. Base catches Flyer's back and legs in cradle.
   Back Spot steps into support head and neck

Stunt Explanation

This stunt starts with Back arch on page 180.

Base

Base has Flyer overhead with Right hand on the small of Flyer's back and Base's left hand on Flyer's left ankle. Base squats and drives Flyer's body upward while also pulling Flyer's left leg into Base's chest region and placing Base's right hand under Flyer's seat

Flyer

Flyer starts in Back Arch position and as Base squats and drives Flyer's back upward, Flyer crunches stomach muscles and pulls upper body up into sitting position. Base will place Bases right hand under Flyer's seat to allow Flyer to execute chair ending position in High V.

Back Spot

Back Spot stands at back right corner of Base and is there to assist if any problems occur. Back Spot can help lock Bases arm out if needed.

Back Arch to Chair

1. Start in Back Arch

2. Flyer stays tight as Base squats
   Base retains grip on Flyer's left ankle

3. Base's right hand moves
   to Flyer's seat, as Flyer sits upright

4. Flyer hits Stunt and Base turns forward.

182

Stunt Explanation

Base

Base starts by holding Flyer in a cradle position, one arm supporting back and the other under Flyer's legs. On count, Base squats and drives Flyer upward using legs, as Base snaps biceps into upward position throwing Flyer up toward ceiling. As Flyer rides and twists, Base keeps eyes on hips, and arms up, waiting to catch Flyer. As Flyer descends Base pulls Flyer in and returns Flyer to cradle.

Flyer

Flyer starts in cradle with arms around Base's shoulders. On count, as Base squats and drives, Flyer rides up and pulls arms to the left to rotate a 360 degree roll. Flyer stops rotating and returns to cradle position, again holding Base's shoulders.

Back Spot

Back Spot stands at back right corner of Base and is there to assist if any problems occur. Back Spot visually follows Flyer to assist if Flyer gets popped over Base's Back, ensuring the safety of the head, back, and neck of Flyer. Back Spot can help support cradle if needed.

Log Roll

1. Flyer starts in cradle position. Flyer's arms around Base's shoulders Base supporting back and legs

2. Base squats, Flyer stays tight

3. Base tosses Flyer upwards starting turn

4. Flyer continues turning Base keeps arms up

5. Base catches Flyer in cradle

Stunt Explanation

Grip

Front Pole and Flyer will face each other with Flyer in front of Front Pole. Flyer and Front Pole shake hands with their right hands. Flyer and Front Pole place their left hands on their foreheads with palms out and thumbs down. Flyer and Front Pole then extend their left arms and grab hands, keeping left arms up high

Base

Base starts in a squat position. Base's Right hand is on top of Base's left hand, and both hands are kept close to Base's lower belly. As Flyer's right foot steps into Base's hands, Base drives Flyer above Base's head, allowing Flyer to turn 180 degrees counterclockwise. As Base lowers Flyer to shoulder height position, Base releases left hand from Flyer's right foot and grabs left foot.

Front Pole

Front Pole, after gripping hands, stands with feet apart. As Flyer walks past, Front Pole drives right arm up and keeps both of Front Pole's arms locked out above Front Pole's head. Flyer will bear down on Front Pole's arms as Base drives Flyer upward to hands. Once Flyer settles into Base's hands, Front Pole releases left arm from Flyer's left hand and then Front Pole turns clockwise to grab Flyer's right calf. Front Pole then releases Flyer's right hand and Front Pole grabs Flyer's right toe. It is important that Front Pole remains in contact with Flyer for the entire duration of the stunt.

Flyer

Flyer walks toward Base, with Left foot first, and steps with right foot onto Base's hands. On count, both Base and Flyer will squat and Flyer jumps upward and pushes down through Flyer's arms onto Front Pole's arms for stability. As Flyer is driven upward, Flyer will lock right leg out, and turn 180 degrees clockwise. Base grabs Flyer's left foot and settles at shoulder height. Front Pole will release Flyer's left arm and then release Flyer's right arm and Flyer stands straight up to end stunt.

Back Spot

Back Spot is not necessary, but if present, stands at back right corner of Base and is there to assist if any problems occur. Back Spot visually follows Flyer, ensuring the safety of the head, back, and neck of Flyer.

Walk Hands with a Pole

Hand Positions

1. Front Pole on Left, Flyer on Right; Front Pole and Flyer shake right hands

2. Front Pole and Flyer put left hands on forehead, thumbs down, palms out

3. Front Pole and Flyer connect hands with thumbs down

4. (Side View) - Keep distance between arms

Walk Hands with a Pole

Technique

1. Grip set; Flyer walks forward with left foot

2. Flyer steps right foot into Base's hand; Base's grip is right hand on top of left hand

3. Base drives Flyer upward; Flyer puts feet on Base's shoulders

4. Front Pole releases Flyer's left hand

5. Front Pole turns to Base's side; grabbing Flyer's ankle

6. Front Pole releases Flyer's right hand; Front Pole grabs Flyer's ankle

Stunt Explanation

Base

Base stands behind Flyer, and Base will grab Flyer by waist. On count, Base and Flyer will squat. Base throws Flyer upward, driving through legs and extending arms above head, snapping at top. Base will then grab under the Flyer's feet as high as possible and settle to hands position.

Flyer

Flyer stands in front of Base with Flyer's hands on Base's wrists. Flyer then places Flyer's right leg into Toe Pitch's hands. On count, Flyer squats with Base, jumps, and snaps through right leg to pencil position, riding as high as possible, and settles into Base's hands.

Back Spot

Toe Pitch grabs the Flyer's right toe and heel squats and on count, thrusts Flyer above Base's head. Toe Pitch will let go of Flyer's heel once the Flyer is above Base's head. Toe Pitch grabs and supports Flyer's right ankle with Toe Pitch's left hand. The Toe Pitch's right hand can remain on Flyer's right toe or move to Base's right forearm.

Toe Pitch Throw Hands

Positions

1. Base grabs Flyer's waist; Flyer grabs Base's wrists

2. Flyer places right foot on Toe Pitch's hands

3. Toe Pitch squats and grabs Flyer's right foot; Right hand on Flyer's toe, left hand on Flyer's heel

Toe Pitch Throw Hands

Technique

1. Set Grip

2. Base tosses Flyer upward, Back Spot drives Flyer's toe

3. Flyer snaps off Base's wrists; Base releases Flyer

4. Flyer tightens; Base catches Flyer's feet

5. Flyer hits Hands

6. Base squats and drives Flyer upward

7. Base pops Flyer

8. Base catches Flyer and slows Flyer down; Flyer grabs Base's wrist

9. Flyer lands on ground

Stunt Explanation

Base

Base starts with Base's left hand on top of Base's right hands. Flyer steps into Base's hands with Flyer's right foot. On count, Base and Flyer squat and Base drives Flyer upward to Base's shoulder level, allowing Flyer to perform a ¼ turn counterclockwise. At this position, the Base is holding Flyer's right foot at chest level and Base's right hand rides up to hold Flyer's right quad.

Flyer

Flyer starts facing Base and steps into Base's hands with right foot, placing Flyer's hands on Base's shoulders, looking down Base's back. On count, Flyer and Base squat and Flyer drives through Flyer's arms, twisting a ¼ turn counterclockwise. Flyer's right toe will end facing the side, pulling the Flyer's left leg upward into a Torch position. Flyer will continue to turn upper body counterclockwise to face the crowd in ending position.

Back Spot

Back Spot stands at back right corner of Base and is there to assist if any problems occur. Back Spot visually follows Flyer ensuring the safety of the head, back, and neck of Flyer.

Walk Torch

1. Hand grip for Torch

2. Flyer sets grip and foot

3. Flyer and Base squat

4. Base drives Flyer upward; Flyer turns 1/4 turn to her left

5. Base settles right hand at Hands Position with thumb on collarbone and right hand reaches for Flyer's Right quad

6. Flyer hits stunt

Stunt Explanation

Base

Base will grab Flyer by waist. On count, Base and Flyer will squat. Base throws Flyer upward, driving through legs and extending arms above head, snapping at top. Base will then catch under Flyer's right foot, as high as possible, with Base's left hand (thumb in) and Base's right hand grabs Flyer's right quad and settle to hands position with a ¼ turn to right.

Flyer

Flyer will stand in front of Base, with feet together and grabbing wrist's of Base. On count, Flyer will squat with Base and lean on Base ever so lightly. Flyer will jump, keeping weight in wrists of Base. As Base releases Flyer, Flyer snaps away from base and turns Flyer's lower body ¼ turn to the right. Flyer will continue to ride to top, remaining tight. Flyer's lower body will face toward the right, standing on Right leg, with left leg in a liberty position. The Upper body will remain facing forward.

Back Spot

Back Spot stands at back right corner of Base and is there to assist if any problems occur.

Note: this stunt is similar to throw hands except for the ending position. The Base grips the Flyers foot holding the entire foot sideways to chest instead of heel facing chest.

Throw Torch

1. Base grabs Flyer's waist; and Flyer grabs Base's wrists

2. Flyer and Base squat

3. Base throws Flyer up; on way up, Flyer turns 1/4 to the right

4. Flyer hits stunt; Base's Left hand on Right foot, Base's Right hand on Flyer's quad

189

Stunt Explanation

Base

Base starts in a squat position. Base's Right hand is on top of Base's left hand, and both hands are kept close to Base's lower belly. As Flyer's right foot steps into Base's hands, Base drives Flyer above Base's head, allowing Flyer to turn 180 degrees counterclockwise. As Base lowers Flyer to shoulder height position, Base will release left hand from Flyer's right foot and grab left foot. Base keeps eyes on Flyer through entire stunt.

Flyer

Flyer walks toward Base, Left foot first and steps with right foot onto Base's hands and Flyer places hands on Base's shoulders. Flyer will look down Base's backside. Note: it is important for Flyer to be directly on top of Base and in close, for this stunt. The closer you are, the lighter you are. As Base squats, Flyer jumps and pushes through arms and locks out right leg. Flyer will ride above Base's head, and turns clockwise, while Base grabs left foot and settles at shoulder height position.

Back Spot

Back Spot will spot on back left corner of stunt. Back Spot will follow Flyer up, ride, and wait until stunt settles. Once stunt settles, Back Spot will slide to right back corner.

Note: when this stunt goes wrong, more often than not, the Flyer usually falls to the back left corner of the Base, hence why the Back Spot is on the left side.

Walk Hands

Positions

1. Base grabs Flyer's right ankle with Base's right hand under heel

2. Flyer places right foot in Base's hand; Flyer places hands on Base's shoulders

3. Closeup of "Hands" grip

Walk Hands

Technique

1. Set Grip

2. Base squats and drives Flyer upward

3. Flyer rotates toward front as Base continues to drive up

4. Base grabs Flyer's left foot Flyer keeps legs shoulder width apart

5. Flyer hits position

6. Base squats

7. Base pops Flyer off front, catching Flyer at waist. Flyer grabs Base's wrists

8. Base slows Flyer's landing

191

Stunt Explanation

Base

Base puts right hand on top of left hand, keeping both hands near lower belly of body. Base will squat on count as Flyer steps into hands with right leg and puts hands on Base's shoulders. Base squats and drives Flyer above Base's head, through to top. Base lets go of right foot with Left hand and grabs Flyer's left foot at extension and locks arms.

Flyer

Flyer walks toward Base, with Left foot first and steps with right foot onto Base's hands, placing hands on Base's shoulder. Flyer will look down Base's backside. Note: it is important for Flyer to be directly on top of Base and in close for this stunt. The closer you are, the lighter you are. As Base squats, Flyer jumps and pushes through arms and locks out right leg. Flyer will ride above Base's head and turn clockwise, while Base grabs left foot and locks out at extension.

Back Spot

Back Spot will spot on back left corner of stunt. Back Spot will follow Flyer up, ride, and wait until stunt settles. Once stunt settles, Back Spot will slide to right back corner. Back Spot can assist Base, by holding Flyer's waist as Base drives upward.

Note: when this stunt goes wrong, more often than not, the Flyer usually falls to the back left corner of the Base, hence why the Back Spot is on the left side.

Walk Extension

Positions

1. Base grabs Flyer's Right foot with Base's right hand under heel

2. Flyer places right foot in Base's Hand; Flyer places hands on Base's shoulders

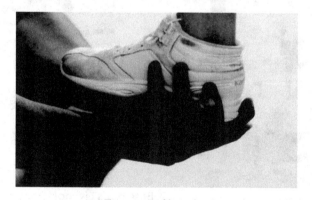

3. Close-up of hand grip

Walk Extension

Technique

1. Set Grip

2. Base squats and drives Flyer upward

3. Flyer rotates toward front as Base continues to drive up

4. Base grabs Flyer's Left foot

5. Base continues to drive Flyer upward to extension

6. Base pops Flyer off front

7. Base grabs Flyer's waist; Flyer grabs Base's wrists, slowing landing

Stunt Explanation

This stunt takes off from the Walk Hands technique see page 190.

Base

Base has Flyer in hands and on count, Base will squat and pop Flyer upward and begin to turn Flyer counterclockwise. Base supports Flyer under right foot with the Base's right hand. Base's Left hand supports under Base's Right Hand (same grip of load in for Walk Hands). Base will lower Flyer to the surface, in a controled manner. Base will squat on count as Flyer puts hands on Base's shoulders, and drives Flyer's foot above head turning clockwise. As Base lowers Flyer to shoulder height position Base will release left hand from Flyer's right foot and grab left foot.

Flyer

Flyer starts facing forward in hands position. On count, Base will squat and drive Flyer upward and Flyer will turn counterclockwise, keeping all weight in right leg, with leg locked. Flyer will place hands on Base's shoulders and tap left leg on floor, keeping all weight on Base's shoulders. As Base squats and Flyer taps floor with Left leg, Flyer bounces and pushes through arms and locks out right leg. Flyer will ride above Base's head and turns clockwise, while Base grabs left foot and settles at shoulder height position in ending position.

Back Spot

Back Spot will spot on back left corner of stunt. Back Spot will follow Flyer down, and possibly assist under Flyer's seat with a forearm pop OR by holding at waist and helping to drive Flyer back up. Once stunt settles, Back Spot will slide to right back corner.

Double Take

1. Stunt starts in Hands Position

4. Base turns Flyer

5. Base lowers Flyer, Flyer locks leg out

8. Base drives Flyer up and turns Flyer

9. Flyer turns and Base grabs Flyers Left foot

194

2. Base squats

3. Base pops Flyer to adjust hand grip

6. Flyer taps ground and pushes off

7. Base drives Flyer upward

10. Settle into Stunt

Stunt Explanation

This stunt is similar to a double take, but instead of turning clockwise, (back the way the stunt went up), this stunt turns counterclockwise. This stunt begins with Walk Hands on page 190.

Base

Base has Flyer in Hands at shoulder level, squats and drives Flyer upward turning Flyer clockwise. The Base's right hand will support left hand, once leaving Flyer's right foot. Base will lower Flyer down to floor on left leg, squat on count as Flyer puts hands on Base's shoulders and drives Flyer's foot above head turning clockwise. As Base lowers Flyer to shoulder height position, Base will release right hand from Flyer's left foot and grab right foot to settle in hands.

Flyer

Flyer starts facing forward in hands position. On count, Base will squat and drive Flyer upward and Flyer will turn clockwise, keeping all weight in left leg, with leg locked. Flyer will place hands on Base's shoulders and tap right leg on floor keeping all weight on Base's shoulders. As Base squats and Flyer taps floor, Flyer bounces and pushes through arms and locks out left leg. Flyer will ride above Base's head and turn counterclockwise, while Base grabs right foot and settles at shoulder height position in ending position.

Back Spot

Back Spot will spot on back left corner of stunt. Back Spot will follow Flyer down, and possibly assist under Flyer's seat with a forearm pop or by holding at waist and helping to drive Flyer back up. Once stunt settles, Back Spot will slide to right back corner.

Around The World

1. Flyer starts in Hands Position

4. Flyer places hands on Base's shoulders

5. Flyer puts right leg on floor

8. Flyer rotates as Base drives Flyer up

9. Flyer finishes rotating

196

Around The World

2. Flyer picks up left foot

3. Flyer turns as Base lowers Flyer

6. Flyer pushes off Base's shoulders

7. Flyer turns as Base drives Flyer upward

10. Flyer hits stunt

Stunt Explanation

Base

Base starts facing Flyer, Base's right hand on top of Base's left hand. On count, Flyer will step into Base's hands with Flyer's right foot. Base and Flyer then squat and Base drives Flyer 6 to 8 inches above Base's head. Base will then release Flyer's right foot and catch Flyer's feet as high as possible in a reverse hands grip, with Base's hands holding the middle of Flyer's feet. Base will then settle stunt at shoulder level.

Flyer

Flyer starts facing Base. On count, Flyer will walk toward Base and place Flyer's right foot into Base's hands, while placing Flyer's hands on Base's shoulders. Base and Flyer squat, and as Base drives Flyer upward, Flyer locks out right leg and pushes off Base's shoulders. Flyer must also slightly lean forward for balance.

Note: When learning this stunt, Flyers usually leans forward enough to cause the Flyer to fall away from the Base. Make sure Flyer says tight and leans into Base.

Back Spot

Back Spot starts shoulder to shoulder with Base, facing Base. If problems occur, the Back Spot can move and follow Flyer forward or backward for best spotting angles.

Walk Reverse Hands

1. Flyer sets grip and foot

2. Flyer and Base squat

3. Base starts to drive; Flyer pushes off Base's shoulders to lock out leg

4. Flyer's leg is locked and Flyer rides up 6 to 8 inches above Base's head, Base releases Flyer

5. Base catches Flyer in Reverse Hands Position; Flyer hits stunt

Stunt Explanation

Base

Base starts with hands on Flyer's waist, and on count, Base and Flyer squat. Base throws Flyer upward, driving through legs and extending arms above head, snapping at top. During the throw, the Base will begin to turn Flyer 180 degrees by pulling with Base's right hand and pushing left hand away. Base will then catch under Flyer's foot at above Base's head and settle to reverse Hands position. Flyer's toes will be facing Base's shoulder, so Base must push harder on Flyer's heels to keep Flyer from falling backward off the front of the stunt.

Flyer

Flyer will stand in front of Base, with feet together, and grab wrist's of Base behind Flyer's back. On count, Flyer will squat with Base and lean on Base ever so lightly. Flyer will jump, keeping weight in wrists of Base. As Base releases Flyer, Flyer will cross right hand through to left hip to complete a half turn and end facing the Base. Flyer will continue to ride to top and separate legs 6 inches, but remaining tight and leaning forward to prevent falling backward off front.

Back Spot

Back Spot stands at back right corner of Base and is there to assist if any problems occur.

Throw Reverse
Side

1. Base grabs Flyer's waist and Flyer grabs base's wrists

2. Base and Flyer squat

3. Base drives Flyer upward; turning Flyer

4. Flyer faces Backward as Base grabs Flyer's feet

5. Flyer hits end position

Throw Reverse
Front

1. Set Grip; Base and Flyer squat

2. Base drives Flyer upward; turning Flyer

3. Flyer continues to rotate to face backward

4. Base grabs under Flyer's feet

5. Flyer hits end position

Stunt Explanation

This stunt starts from Reverse Hands Position on Page 196.

Base

Base starts with Flyer in reverse hands. Base will move left hand to the ball of the Flyer's right foot and drive Flyer's right foot upward to Hitch Position, attempting to lock arm. On count, Base will squat and drive with Right arm, locking Base's Left Arm and popping Flyer's left leg upward. As Flyer brings right foot to Liberty Position, Base grabs the Flyer's right heel and locks out the Right arm and completes 180 degree turn clockwise.

Flyer

Flyer starts in Hands Position, at Prep Level and facing Backwards. As Base squats and drives, the Flyer will pick up the right leg and end in Hitch Position. On count, the Base will drive Flyer's left leg upward and Flyer will lock out right leg. In addition, Flyer will also turn clockwise 180 degrees and pull left leg up to knee for Liberty Position.

Note: when attempting twisting tricks – Over rotation is a common problem, to counter this do not pull hard enough to complete the full/half twist, allow the momentum of the trick to finish the twist.

Back Spot

Back Spot will start spotting from the left corner and will slide to the back right corner once stunt hits.

1. Base grabs Flyer's waist; Flyer grabs Base's wrists

2. Base tosses Flyer upward

3. Flyer turns 180 degrees

4. Base catches Flyer's Feet

5. Flyer hits position

1. Base and Flyer squat

2. Base drives Flyer upward

3. Flyer turns 180 degrees

4. Flyer settles in at shoulder level

5. Base drives Left arm up

6. Base squats and drives right arm up

7. Base releases Flyer's left foot and puts both hands on Flyer's Right foot

Stunt Explanation

Base

Base will grab Flyer by waist. On count, Base and Flyer will squat. Base throws Flyer upward, driving through legs and extending arms above head, snapping at top. Base will then catch under Flyer's feet as high as possible and settle to hands position.

Flyer

Flyer will stand in front of Base, with feet together, grabbing wrist's of Base. On count, Flyer will squat with Base and lean on Base ever so lightly. Flyer will jump, keeping weight in wrists of Base. After Base releases Flyer, Flyer will continue to ride to top and open legs about 6 to 8 inches apart, but remain tight. Flyer will always keep head up.

Back Spot

Back Spot stands at back right corner of Base and is there to assist if any problems occur.

Throw Hands
Front View

1. Base grabs Flyer's waist; Flyer grabs Base's wrists. Base and Flyer squat

2. Base tosses Flyer upward; Flyer snaps off Base's wrists

3. Base settles into position

4. Flyer hits Stunt

Throw Hands

Side View

1. Base grabs Flyer's waist and Flyer grabs Base's wrists.

2. Base and Flyer squat

3. Base tosses Flyer upward; Flyer snaps off Base's wrists

4. Base grabs Flyer's feet

5. Base settles into position

6. Base pops Flyer upward

7. Base catches Flyer's waist; Flyer grabs Base's wrists

8. Base slows Flyers landing

Stunt Explanation

Bases

Base stands behind Flyer. Base grabs Flyers hands in position 1. On count, Flyer and Base squat, Base and Flyer then flip handgrip to position 2, as Base lifts Flyer upward. Base continues to drive through Base's legs and arms, driving Flyer upward, above Base's head, until Flyer's feet are comfortably on Base's shoulders. Base releases right hand, grabs upper calf, and pulls down. Repeat same for left hand and calf. The Base needs to keep head up for support.

Flyer

Flyer stands with feet together, arms at side with hands behind and palms up, fingers back. Base grabs and connects with Flyer's hand grip. On count, Flyer squats and jumps up flipping handgrip to position 2, flipping the wrists so that Flyer can now push against the Base's hands. If the wrists don't flip, the Flyer will not be able to support her own weight. As Flyer drives through the arms, the Flyer should keep elbows locked, and pull hips up. Flyer keeps weight on arms as much as possible, until feet are able to be placed in the correct position on Base's shoulders. Flyer releases right hand and then left as Base secures legs. To tighten the position, the Flyer should lock heels together behind Base's head, hitting end position.

Back Spot

Back Spot spots back right corner of Base. Back Spot is there to aid and assist if any problems occur.

Purdue Up

Positions

1. Set Grip

2. Hand Position 1

3. Hand Position 2 - Base gets under Flyer

Purdue Up

1. Base and Flyer squat

2. Flyer keeps arms and feet together during drive upward

3. Flyer pulls hips up

4. Flyer settles into Shoulder Stand, placing feet on Base's shoulders

5. Flyer hits end position

Stunt Explanation

Base

Base will grab Flyer by waist. On count, Base and Flyer will squat. Base throws Flyer upward, driving through legs and extending arms above head, snapping at top. After Base snaps, his head should be looking straight forward. Flyer should ride up and land on shoulders where Base will guide Flyer's legs and grab the tops of Flyer's calves and pull down.

NOTE - The Difference between this and all other "Throw Tricks" is that Base does not want to look up at Flyer in this trick. Looking up will cause the shoulders to not be in the correct spot for landing and therefore, making the stunt harder.

Flyer

Flyer stands in front of Base, with feet together and grabbing wrists of Base. On count, Flyer will squat leaning on Base ever so lightly. Flyer will jump, keeping weight in wrists of Base. After Base releases, Flyer will continue to ride to top and open legs 6-8 inches apart. Flyer will stay tight and settle in when feet land on shoulders, Hitting end position – High V.

Back Spot

Back Spot stands at back right corner of Base and is there to assist if any problems occur.

Throw Shoulder Stand

1. Set grip

2. Flyer and Base squat

3. Base throws Flyer through to top. Base keeps head forward.

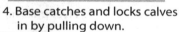

4. Base catches and locks calves in by pulling down.

5. Flyer hits stunt.

Throw Shoulder Stand

Stunt Explanation

Base

Base will grab Flyer by waist. On count, Base and Flyer will squat. Base throws Flyer upward, driving through legs and extending arms above head, snapping at top. Base will then catch under Flyer's feet as high as possible and settle to hands position. Base then squats keeping elbows up (so Flyer doesn't fall forward), and drives Flyer upward to extension.

Flyer

Flyer will stand in front of Base, with feet together, grabbing wrist's of Base, behind Flyer's back. On count, Flyer will squat with Base and lean on Base ever so lightly. Flyer will jump, keeping weight in wrists of Base. After Base releases Flyer, Flyer will continue to ride to top and open legs about 6 inches apart, while remaining tight. As Base pumps, Flyer will keep head up and stay tight to hit end position.

Back Spot

Back Spot stands at back right corner of Base and is there to assist if any problems occur. Back Spot can help lock Bases arm out if needed.

Pump n Go Hands

1. Base and Flyer squat

4. Base settles in Hands position

5. Base squats

Pump n Go Hands

2. Base tosses Flyer upward;
   Flyer snaps off Base's wrists

3. Base grabs Flyer's Feet

6. Base drives Flyer upward

7. Flyer hits end position

Stunt Explanation

Base

Base will grab Flyer by waist. On count, Base and Flyer will squat. Base throws Flyer upward, driving through legs and extending arms above head, snapping at top. Base will then catch under Flyer's feet at extension level.
If the throw is not high enough, the Base can catch feet on way up (as long as Flyer is on way up) until technique improves.

Flyer

Flyer will stand in front of Base, with feet together, grabbing wrist's of Base. On count, Flyer will squat with Base and lean on Base ever so lightly. Flyer will jump, keeping weight in wrists of Base. After Base releases Flyer, Flyer will continue to ride to top and open legs about 6 to 8 inches apart, while remaining tight.

Back Spot

Back Spot stands at back right corner of Base and is there to assist if any problems occur.

Throw Extension

1. Base and Flyer squat

2. Base drives Flyer upward

3. Base grabs Flyer's feet and continues driving up

4. Flyer hits end position

212

Stunt Explanation

Base

Base will grab Flyer by waist. On count, Base and Flyer will squat. Base throws Flyer upward, driving through legs and extending arms above head, snapping at top. Base will then catch under Flyer's foot at extension level. Base will catch Flyer's heel with right hand and the Base's left hand will grab under the Flyer's toe, supporting the ball of foot.

Note: When learning this technique, it is very common to grip Flyer's foot with the hamburger grip (thumb under ball of foot and rest of fingers are on top of foot, as with holding burger and eating it). This is incorrect and Base will struggle with this technique.

Flyer

Flyer will stand in front of Base, with feet together, grabbing wrist's of Base, behind Flyer's back. On count, Flyer will squat with Base and lean on Base ever so lightly. Flyer will jump, keeping weight in wrists of Base. After Base releases Flyer, Flyer will continue to ride to top and pull one leg up for a 1 legged trick, while remaining tight.

Back Spot

Back Spot stands at back right corner of Base and is there to assist if any problems occur.

1. Base and Flyer squats

2. Base throws Flyer upward

3. Base catches one of Flyer's Feet; Flyer puts all wieght on that foot.

1. Liberty

2. Scale

3. Heel Stretch

4. Bow and Arrow

5. Scorpion

6. Scale

Stunt Explanation

This stunt starts at Hands position on page 190.

Base

Base has Flyer in Hands position and baby pops Flyer upward to adjust right hand grip, moving Right hand to Flyer's ball of foot from Flyer's heel. On count, Base squats and drives Flyer up, turning Flyer's right toe to the right while at the same time taking Base's left hand and supporting Flyer's right heel with thumb facing forward, driving Flyer upward. Base keeps body facing forward as Flyer turns and hits High Torch Arabesque.

Note: Keep Flyer over Base's nose as driving up.

Flyer

Flyer starts in hands position. On count, as Base drives Flyer upward, Flyer turns ¼ turn to the right and pulls left leg up to arabesque. Flyer needs to keep weight in ball of foot throughout drive and arabesque.

Note: To prevent from falling do not lean into the lift, as Base drives.

Back Spot

Back Spot stands at back right corner of Base and is there to assist if any problems occur.

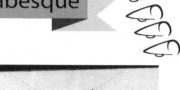

High Torch Arabesque

1. Flyer hits Hands Position

2. Base squats

3. Flyer starts to turn to Arabesque; Base grabs Flyer's heel with left hand to support grip

4. Flyer hits stunt

High Torch Arabesque

3. Base drives Flyer upward

4. Flyer snaps at top of throw

7. Flyer starting to turn to Arabesque;
   Base grabs Flyer's heel with left hand
   to support grip

8. Flyer hits stunt

Stunt Explanation

Base

Base starts with hands on Flyer's waist. On count, Base and Flyer squat. Base throws Flyer upward, driving through legs and extending arms above head, snapping at top. Base will then catch under Flyer's right foot at extension level. Base will catch Flyer's heel with right hand and the Base's left hand will grab under the Flyer's toe, supporting the ball of foot.

Note: When learning this technique, it is very common to grip Flyer's foot with the hamburger grip (thumb under ball of foot and rest fingers are on top of foot, as with holding burger and eating it). This is incorrect.

Flyer

Flyer will stand in front of Base, with feet together, grabbing wrist's of Base. On count, Flyer will squat with Base and lean on Base ever so lightly. Flyer will jump, keeping weight in wrists of Base, into a tuck position. After Base releases Flyer, Flyer will continue to ride to top and will open out of tuck position into the Heel Stretch position, being careful not to stomp down on Base, but to pull up through rib cage, which makes Flyer lighter.

Back Spot

Back Spot stands at back right corner of Base and is there to assist if any problems occur.

Ball Up Stretch

1. Base grabs Flyer's waist; Flyer grabs Base's wrists

2. Flyer and Base squats

5. Base releases Flyer

218

Ball Up Stretch

3. Base drives Flyer upward

4. Base drives Flyer up
   in tuck position

6. Flyer extends legs and
   Base catches Flyers right leg

7. Flyer catches foot in
   Heel Stretch Position

Stunt Explanation

Base

Base starts with hands on Flyer's waist and on count, Base and Flyer squat. Base throws Flyer upward, driving through legs and extending arms above head, snapping at top. During the throw, the Base will begin to turn Flyer 360 degrees by pulling with Base's right hand and pushing left hand away. Base will then catch under Flyer's feet above Base's head and drive to extension, locking arms. (This trick can also be caught 1 footed)

Flyer

Flyer will stand in front of Base, with feet together, grabbing wrist's of Base, behind Flyer's back. On count, Flyer will squat with Base and lean on Base ever so lightly. Flyer will jump keeping weight in wrists of Base. As Base releases Flyer, Flyer will cross right hand through to left hip and Flyer's left hand snaps down behind Flyer's right hip, to complete a full turn and end facing the front. Flyer will continue to ride to top and separate legs 6 inches, while remaining tight and leaning forward to prevent falling off front.

Note; As Flyer twists up, keep hips and shoulders square to keep rotation stratight.

Back Spot

Back Spot stands at back right corner of Base and is there to assist if any problems occur.

Throw 360 UP

Front

1. Set Grip; Base and Flyer squat

2. Base drives Flyer upward begining rotation

3. Base reaches for Flyer's feet as rotation continues

4. Base grabs Flyer's feet and drives Flyer upward

5. Flyer hits end position.

1. Base and Flyer squat

2. Base drives Flyer upward, begining rotation

3. Base reaches for Flyer's feet as rotation continues

4. Base grabs Flyer's feet and drives Flyer upward

5. Flyer hits end position

Stunt Explanation

Base

Base starts facing front with the Flyer's right heel in Base's Right hand and Base's left hand will grab underneath the upper thigh of Flyer's right leg. On count, the Flyer and Base will squat, and Base drives left hand up, keeping hand close to body, until Flyer is in an upright position. As this occurs, Base also drives Flyer's right foot upward and begins a ¾ clockwise turn with Flyer. At completion of turn, Base puts Left hand under Flyer's right toe, locking arm and ending stunt with Flyer in Liberty Position.

Flyer

Flyer starts standing on left side of Base at a 90 degree angle. Flyer lifts right leg off floor and places in Base's hands. Flyer keeps hands at side. On count, Base and Flyer squat, Flyer jumps upward, allowing Base to pull Flyer into Base and in an upright position. It is important that the Flyer's leg remains locked to execute this stunt. Once the Flyer is upright, Base drives Flyer's right foot upward. The Flyer remains tight as the Base turns the flyer in a ¾ clockwise turn. Flyer then pulls Left Leg upward into a Liberty Position to end the Stunt, also hitting the end position – High V.

Back Spot

Back Spot stands at back right corner of Base and is there to assist if any problems occur. Back Spot may also assist this stunt by holding Flyer's waist to load stunt and then moving to back right corner from the back of the Base.

"J" UP

1. Base grabs Flyer's inner thigh and ankle

2. Flyer squats

3. Base drives Flyer's leg under Flyer

4. Flyer turns as Base puts hands under Flyer's feet

5. Base grabs Flyer's right foot and drives upward

6. Flyer hits end position

Stunt Explanation

Base

Base starts with Flyer in front of Base. Base's right hand shakes Flyer's right hand, then connect Base's left hand to Flyer's Left hand, both with thumbs down.

Flyer places Right foot onto forearm of Base's Right arm. On count, Base and Flyer will squat and pop forearm. Base will drive Flyer upward, locking arms above head until Flyer lands with feet on Base's right shoulder. During this process, Base keeps arms as close to Base's ears as possible after pop. After landing, Base will squat and drive Flyer upward, using legs, and then pops Flyer upward, releasing Flyer's hand so Flyer's feet can be caught by Base's right hand, in a Cupie position, above Base's head.

Flyer

Base starts with Flyer in front of Base. Base's right hand shakes Flyer's right hand, then connect Base's left hand to Flyer's Left hand, both with thumbs down.

Flyer places right foot into forearm of Bases right arm. On count, Flyer and Base will squat. On drive, Flyer will snap off right leg and drive upward, locking and pushing through arms to hips up position keeping as much weight on Bases arms as possible, while placing both of Flyer's feet on Base's right shoulder. Base will squat again and drive Flyer upward. Flyer will release hands of Base, stand upright and tight, to enable Base to grab both of Flyer's feet in Base's right hand. Flyer remains tight throughout entire stunt.

Back Spot

Back Spot stands at back right corner of Base and is there to assist if any problems occur. Back Spot visually follows Flyer, ensuring the safety of the head, back, and neck of Flyer. Back Spot can help assist with Flyer's feet landing on Base's Right shoulder and help lock arms of Base if needed.

Tarzan

1. Flyer sets grip and foot

4. Base pops forearm. Flyer snaps off and presses through arms

7. Base drives Flyer, and releases hands

2. Flyer puts right foot on Base's arm

3. Base and Flyer squat

5. Flyer settles on Right shoulder of Base

6. Base squats

8. Flyer starts to pull legs together;
Base gets hands in place for grip

8. Flyer hits stunt (i.e.Cupie)

Stunt Explanation

Base

Base starts with hands on Flyer's back and hips, and on count, Base and Flyer will squat and Flyer jumps. Base will drive Flyer upward, directly overhead, and through a Back tuck position, extending Base's arms up as high as Base can reach. As Flyer descends, Base grabs Flyer's feet and locks out final stunt in extension. This stunt can also be caught with one foot or in prep position.

Flyer

Flyer starts with feet together and arms in low "V" position. On count, Flyer will squat, execute a spotted standing back tuck, rotating up and in front of Base. As Base grabs Flyer's feet, Flyer should extend and lock out legs, being careful not to stomp, but pull up through legs.

Note: When attempting this trick - Do not over or under rotate! Stand up at end of stunt.

Back Spot

Back Spot stands on right side even with or slightly in front of the Base. If Flyer under rotates, Back Spot can assist in the landing of the stunt by supporting belly at waist. If Flyer over rotates, Back Spot supports back and waist of Flyer helping to control landing -feet first. Back Spot can also help lock Base out if throw is not high enough.

Rewind

Positions

1. Base puts hands on Flyer's lower back

2. Flyer stands with feet together arms Low "V"

3. Base pushes into Flyer's lower back as Base squats

1. Set Grip Base squats

2. Flyer jumps and tucks and Base drives Flyer up

3. Base controls Flyer

4. Flyer begins to rotate

5. Flyer drives Flyer Up and releases

6. Flyer rotates in tuck

7. Base gets under Flyer's Feet and extends arms

STUNTING

GLOSSARY

Glossary

Awesome: A single or multi-based stunt in which the Base holds the Flyer with feet together on the Base's hand(s) in an Extended Position. In Co-ed stunts, this also refers to when the Base has the Flyer in one hand and the other hand is extended in a High "V"

Back Spot: A person that stands at the Back of the stunt. This person will assist with the loading and catching in multi-based stunts or at the back and side of a Single Based stunt. In addition, the Back Spot is responsible to help protect the head, neck, and back of the Flyer during the stunt.

Ball Up: A release and catch move where the Flyer starts standing upright, is tossed upwards in a tuck position, and returns to an upright standing position, and is caught by the Base . Example: Ball Up Stretch.

Ball – X: A skill executed during a Basket Toss/Cradle in which the Flyer starts in a tuck position and goes to an "X" Position.

Base: A person(s) that holds, lifts, tosses, and catches a Flyer into and out of a stunt.

Basket Toss: A release move where 2 Bases have interlocking grips. There can be up to 4 Bases involved in a toss, with the back Base being responsible for the safety of the Flyer's head, neck, and back.

Brace: A person(s) that are physically connected to the Flyer for stability.

Braced Flip: A transitional stunt that when executed, the Flyer will rotate hip-over head, while connected hand to hand with 2 Bases.

Cradle: A release move in which the Bases and Back Spot wait with palms up, to catch the Flyer. It is usually executed to enable the Flyer to get out of a stunt and return to the ground. The Flyer will land in a Pike Position, with the Base's arms catching under the Flyer's Back and thighs.
There are 2 types: Traditional and Hollow Body.

Co-ed Stunts: Stunts typically performed by a Male Base and a Female Flyer, but can be performed by all Females or all Males and are also referred to as single based stunts.

Cupie: A single or multi-based stunt in which the Base holds the Flyer with feet together on the Base's hand(s) in an Extended Position. In Co-ed stunts this also refers to when the Base has the Flyer in one hand and the other hand is on the Base's hip.

Dead Leg: Refers to a Flyer's leg when there is no weight on it and it is not being supported by a Base(s). This is a transitional step and leads into a 1 legged stunt.

Dismount: A method to get out of a stunt. See Cradle and Pencil Drop.

Downward Inversion: A skill where the Flyer is inverted, head down and feet up, and is moving toward the ground. Such a skill would be a Waterfall.

Downward Motion: The movement of the Flyer toward the ground.

Elevator: In a stunt, this is when the Flyer is extended upward to the Bases' shoulder level, also called Prep Position.

Extended Position: A skill in which the Bases' arms are extended with arms locked while supporting a Flyer.

Extended Stunt: A stunt in which the Bases' arms are extended with arms locked while supporting a Flyer who is in an upright body position.

Flat Back: A stunt in which the Flyer is supported by the Bases under shoulders, legs, and back. The Flyer is in a supine position (lying on their back).

Flyer: In a stunt group or basket toss, this is the person that is building and that is supported by the Bases.

Free-Flipping Mount: Immediately prior to the stunt, the entry into a stunt where the top person passes through an inverted position without physical contact with a base, brace, or the performing surface.

Front Spot: In a stunt group, this is the person that stands in front of the stunt, usually facing the Flyer, and is there to provide additional support to the stunt group.

Full: A 360 degree twisting rotation.

Full-Up: A stunt in which the Flyer executes a 360 degree turn before hitting the ending position. This is not a flip. The Flyer rotates with assistance of Bases by turning the Flyer's foot as the Flyer is extended to a Prep or Extension Position.

Ground: Is the surface from which the stunts start and typically return to.

Half: In a stunt, this is when the Flyer is extended upward to the Bases' shoulder level, also called Prep Position or Elevator.

Hamburger Grip: An INCORRECT grip; when the Base's fingers are on the top of Flyer's shoe and Base's thumb is under Flyer's toe.

Hand/Arm Connection: Is the physical contact of a Flyer and Bases in which the hand is touching/grabbing the others arm.

Handstand: A straight body position, in which the hands are placed on the ground, arms extended and the body is extended straight upward over the head.

Hollow Body Cradle: A release move in which the Bases and Back Spot wait with palms up, to catch the Flyer. It is usually executed to enable the Flyer to get out of a stunt and return to the ground. The Flyer will land in a Hollow Body Position, with her chin tucked in, and the Flyer's arms on her thighs. The Bases' arms will catch under the Flyer's back and thighs.

Inversion: The act of being inverted.

Inverted: A skill where the Flyer's shoulders are below the waist and the feet are over the head.

Jump: A skill in which the individual will propel themselves upward into the air using the power in the lower extremities for height.

Kick Basket: A skill executed during a Basket Toss/Cradle in which the Flyer starts in a straight position and kicks with one leg.

Kick Double Full: A skill executed during a Basket Toss/Cradle in which the Flyer starts in a straight position and kicks with one leg to initiate 2 360 degree rotations or 2 Full turns.

Kick Full: A skill executed during a Basket Toss/Cradle in which the Flyer starts in a straight position and kicks with one leg to initiate a 360 degree rotation or 1 Full turn

Leap Frog: A skill in which the Flyer will move from one location to another by moving over a Front Spot and between the Front Spot's arms maintaining contact the entire time. The Flyer can either move to a new set of Bases or the original Bases will move forward to re-catch the Flyer.

Liberty: A position of the Flyer in which one leg is being held by the Base(s) and the other leg is bent at the knee, with the Flyer's toe touching the calf/knee of Flyer's other leg.

Load In: Is how a Flyer starts a stunt; placing 1 or both feet on the hands of the Base(s) before performing the stunt.

Log Roll: A release move in which the Flyer will execute a full turn in a horizontal position.

Mount: Can also be referred to as a Stunt; a skill in which a Flyer is supported by a Base or Bases.

Multi-based Stunt: A skill in which a Flyer is supported by multiple Bases.

Original Base(s): Is the Base or Bases that started the stunt with the Flyer.

On Count: Timing relative to building or executing a skill.

Pencil Drop: A release trick, in which the Bases and Back Spot catch the Flyer's at waist level. It is usually executed to enable the Flyer to get out of a stunt and return to the ground; especially good for beginner levels. The Flyer puts feet and hands together and stays in a straight body position to land on the ground.

Pendulum/Pendulum Style: When the top person falls, either forward or backward, away from the vertical axis (usually landing in a flat-bodied position) and is caught by additional Bases.

Pike: A body position in which the legs are kept together and brought up towards the body at a 90 degree angle, forming a "L".

Position 1: Is the position of the hands of the Bases. The hands are held at hip level with palms up, fingers facing the opposing Base and gripping the Flyer's toe and heel.

Position 2: Is the position of the hands of the Bases. The hands are held at or above shoulder height, palms up and fingers facing outward with fingers gripping the front of the toe and the back of the heel.

Prep-Level: A skill in which the Bases' arms are held at shoulder height to support the Flyer.

Prep Position: In a stunt, this is when the Flyer is extended upward to the Bases' shoulder level, also called Prep Position or Elevator.

Primary Support: Is the Base of the stunt that is supporting the majority of the Flyer's weight.

Prone Position: A body position in which the body is straight and in a face down position on the stomach.

Release Move: A skill in which the Flyer becomes disconnected from the Base(s) and returns to the Base(s) at the completion of the skill. Co-ed and Transitional moves are the most common.

Re-load: Is when the Flyer leaves the Base's hands and returns both Flyer's feet to the original Bases' hands to Load In Position.

Rewind: A stunt in which the Flyer leaves the ground and performs a back tuck with assistance from the Base and lands with feet on the group or Main Base's hands.

Second Level: A skill in which the Bases' arms are held at shoulder height to support the Flyer.

Set: To prepare to build or execute a skill.

Show and Go: A transitional stunt in which the Flyer starts in the loading position, is extended over the head of the Bases through the Extension Position and returns to the load in position.

Shoulder Stand: A stunt in which the Flyer has both feet on the shoulders of the Base.

Shoulder Stand Level: A skill in which the Bases arms are held at shoulder height to support the Flyer.

Single-Based Double Awesome/Cupie: A Single Based stunt in which the Base is holding 2 Flyers. Each Flyer has both feet in one of the Hands of the Base.

Single-Based Stunt: A skill in which a Flyer is supported by a single Base.

Single-Leg Stunt: A stunt in which the Flyer is supported by a Base(s) with only 1 leg being held by the Base(s).

SLT: Stands for Step, Lock, Tighten. This refers to when a Flyer steps into position, puts pressure on the leg to straighten it out, lock the leg in this position, and tightens up all the muscles in the body to hold the position

Sponge: A skill in which the Flyer is standing in the Base(s) hands in Position 1. The Flyer is in a tuck position with their hands on Base's shoulders to support Flyer's own weight.

Sponge Toss: A release move in which the Flyer is held in Position 1, tossed upward, and released ending up in a cradle.

Squish: A skill in which the Flyer is standing in the Base(s) hands in Position 1. The Flyer is in a tuck position with their hands on Base's shoulders to support Flyer's own weight.

Straddle Position: A position in which the lower extremities are brought up toward the upper body at a 90 degree angle, similar to a Pike Position. However, the Legs are separated, one leg on each side of the body.

Straddle Sit: A stunt in which the Flyer is held in a straddle position by the Bases, also called Teddy Bear.

Straight Cradle: A release move from a stunt in which the Flyer lands in a cradle after being released from the Bases without executing any additional skills.

Straight Ride: A skill executed during a Basket Toss/Cradle in which the Flyer starts in a straight position and cradles.

Stunt: Can also be referred to as a Mount; a skill in which a Flyer is supported by a Base or Bases.

Supine Position: A body position in which the body is straight and the face is facing upward.

Suspended Flip/Roll: A transitional stunt in which the Flyer performs a flipping motion while maintaining contact with the Base(s).

Three Quarter (3/4) Front Flip (stunt): A forward hip-over-head rotation from an upright position to a cradle position.

Teddy Bear: A stunt in which the Flyer is held in a straddle position by the Bases, also called Straddle Sit.

Tick-Tock: A stunt in which the Flyer starts out being held by the Bases on one foot. The Flyer then transfers weight to the other foot, and Bases release the first foot and grab the second foot.

Toe Pitch: Is the person in a single based stunt, who assists the Base by pushing upwards on a Flyer's foot for additional height or support.

Toss: A release move in which the Flyer is launched upward from the Bases and then released.

Traditional Cradle: A release move in which the Bases and Back Spot wait with palms up, to catch the Flyer. It is usually executed to enable the Flyer to get out of a stunt and return to the ground. The Flyer will land in a Pike Position, with the Bases' arms catching under the Flyer's Back and thighs, with the Flyer supporting her own weight by wrapping her arms around the Bases' shoulders.

Transitional Stunt: A skill that connects multiple stunts together.

Tuck Position: A body position in which the knees and hips are bent and closed together, and brought up to the upper body near the chest.

Twist: Is when the body rotates or spins by twisting the hips.

Twisting Stunt: A stunt in which the Flyer executes a twist as the Flyer is driven upwards.

Twisting Toss: A skill executed during a Basket Toss/Cradle in which the Flyer executes a twist.

Two-Leg Stunt: A stunt in which the Flyer is supported by a Base(s) with both legs being held by the Base(s).

V Sit: Is the position in which Cradles are caught. In this body position, the hips are bent at a right angle creating a "V" position.

Splint Technique

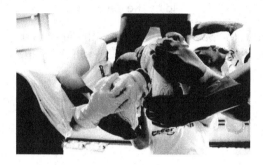

Twist Grip

Hang Drill

Walkin Grip

Hamburger Grip
Incorrect

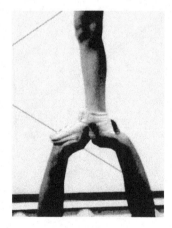

Torch Grip

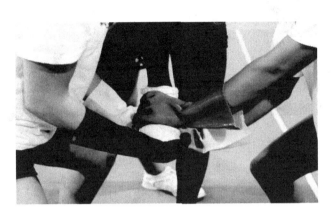

Lib Grip Multiple Bases

Lib Grip Coed

Pole Grip

Lunge

Hip Pocket

Double Lunge

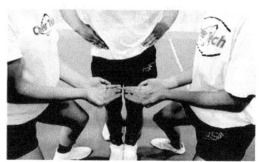

Bases' hand Position 1
Bases' are placed at hip level

Bases hand position 1. Front hand grabs
under Toe, back hand grabs under heel

Base hand position 2
Arms are Close to chest and under foot

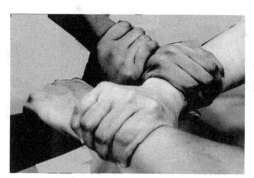

Basket grip for Bases

Special Thanks

Carly

Madison

Jamie

Samantha

Nicole

Paige

Breana

Aubrey

A J